CONFRONTING CHRISTOFASCISM

HEALING THE EVANGELICAL WOUND

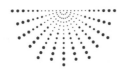

CAROLYN BAKER

APOCRYPHILE
PRESS

Reading this book is not unlike reading other books by survivors of trauma. Only in this case the author is wrestling with a life-time of trauma and recovery around religion, very bad religion, that took over her parents' lives (her parents also being victims of trauma in their past). But the book is not just about the author's harrowing personal journey—she links her story to the common trauma we are undergoing as a nation ever since Donald Trump appeared on the scene—and, with a big lift from evangelicals—rendered fascism fashionable. The author's insights help to explain January 6. She explains from years inside the belly of the beast what sick religion can do to souls and society alike. She reveals why Trump, himself a victim of a traumatic childhood, appeals to his followers so strongly; why QAnon flourishes among evangelicals; how racism is baked in to the evangelical history; how the worldview of "Jesus saves" so takes over a soul that reality itself is sidelined. And thinking. And creation. And justice. And compassion.

—Matthew Fox, author of *Original Blessing* and *One River, Many Wells*

This is a fierce, brilliant, indispensable book by one of our most inspired and lucid guides through our collective dark night. In it, Carolyn Baker weaves together poignant personal testimony and political and spiritual analysis to show us both the terrible danger of Christofascism and the way through and beyond its lethal seductions. Read it and give it to everyone you know who cares about our human future and the future of democracy.

—Andrew Harvey, author of *The Hope: A Guide To Sacred Activism*

Carolyn Baker is a meta-modern surveyor of the psycho-spiritual religious landscape, or at least the particular territory of Western fundamentalism/evangelicalism. Drawing down inspiration from the cultural satellites that orbit, she points the laser locator with unflinching accuracy at the historical context out of which fundamentalism has risen and has come to a dangerous crescendo of political fascism married to fundamentalist religion. Then she turns the laser around. With high doses of vulnerability, she shares her own formative journey in fundamentalism, which parallels my own. Carolyn shows how one can move toward wholeness and healing as one lets go of a story that is way too small and constricting for the soul's longing. Of course the journey does not end. Carolyn, like other healthy pilgrims, recognizes that with curiosity, compassion and courage she continues to explore the mystery of being alive at this threshold time for humanity. Like the poet Rilke, she lives her life "in ever widening circles." She may not complete the last one but she gives herself to it.

—Dr. Terry Chapman, author of *The Sabbath Pause*

With extensive research, careful documentation and analysis and an unflinching look at her own personal history, Carolyn Baker details clearly the foundation laid by Christian theology that undergirds the rise and dominance of Christo-Fascism. She shows that extreme nationalism, violence and terror are natural by products of Christian fundamentalism. It is a must-read for all searching for the way forward.

—Inelle Cox Bagwell, National Board of Directors, United Methodist Women, 1988-1996; Recipient, Gilbert H. Caldwell Justice Ministry Award, Church Within A Church Movement, 2012

Apocryphile Press
1100 County Route 54
Hannacroix, NY 12087
www.apocryphilepress.com

Printed in the United States of America
ISBN 978-1-949643-94-7 | paper
ISBN 978-1-949643-95-4 | ePub

Please join our mailing list at www.apocryphilepress.com/free. We'll keep you up-to-date on all our new releases, and we'll also send you a FREE BOOK. Visit us today!

In memory of my parents, Dean and Olive Baker

"When fascism comes to America,
it will be wrapped in the flag
and carrying a cross."
—attributed to Sinclair Lewis

CONTENTS

FOREWORD

BY FRANK SCHAEFFER

Carolyn Baker has saved me a lot of work. In *Confronting Christofascism: Healing the Evangelical Wound*, she answers two questions I'm asked all the time: "What happened to the evangelicals?" *and* "I'm journeying out of the evangelical community; can you advise me how to do this?" This book answers both questions—frighteningly well.

Making my final break with my evangelical/fundamentalist past in the late 1980s was like turning on some sort of creative tap. As my evangelical leader-father's sidekick I'd been a miniature flash-in-the-pan evangelical leader, with a growing following. Back in the 1970s and early 1980s, I was used to speaking to huge audiences at events such as the Southern Baptist pastors' convention; the annual meeting of the National Religious Broadcasters; Dr. Kennedy's church in Coral Gables, Florida; Jerry Falwell's church and college in Lynchburg, Virginia; and on several nationwide seminar tours where Dad and I packed auditoriums. My evangelical books sold by the pallet load, whereas my secular books (since) have sold as individual copies.

But as an artist and writer, I also knew that even if I could have kept putting up with the "theology"—which I couldn't—let alone tolerated the insane, hate-filled, gun-toting right-wing politics, the evangelical/fundamentalist subculture is death to artistic creativity. That is because art depends on at least attempted honesty and questioning. So I ran. And this was the better part of forty years before Trump's evangelical and evangelical-enabled thugs stormed the Capitol.

When I left the evangelical/fundamentalist world, I found that I was no longer looking over my shoulder wondering what people would think. You see, an evangelical leader looks powerful, but he makes a bad trade, sort of like Prince Charles. You get the life and the palace, but being Prince Charles is all you'll ever do. You are all wrapper and no candy. It's a gilded cage and you are *stuck*. It's the worst typecasting imaginable. Christian leadership is the only guaranteed way to lose all faith in self, God, and goodness.

As Baker writes in this brilliant book, "I have come to believe that evangelicals do not comprehend what they are reading when they read: 'I turned my heart to know and to search out and to seek wisdom and the scheme of things' (Ecclesiastes 7:25). Because fundamentalist Christianity is so thoroughly obsessed with 'knowing,' there is little room for appreciating or savoring wisdom. Wisdom is not acquired through knowledge or intellect but through the soul. The soul is the crux of our humanity, and all fundamentalists acknowledge that fact, but they view the soul as something that must be 'saved,' rather than the mirror image of the divine within us that we did not acquire and that we cannot 'lose.'"

Concentrating on belief rather than on inner character leads some people—whether atheist or religious—to get stuck on the rules. That is exactly what all fundamentalism is: people mistaking rules, and myths, to enforce a false manmade spiritual goal. And because the mistake is a massive one, all sorts of cruelties and fictions are used to reinforce this and endless training for a salvation... that never comes.

Enter post-9/11 "Christians" stalking the grieving families of soldiers killed in our wars, desecrating the solemnity of their funerals with screams of "God hates fags!" and "God hates America!" and enter Trump's followers. Enter those willing to even turn wearing masks and getting a lifesaving vaccine into culture-war fodder to "own the libs" at the cost of life itself.

There is only one defense against the rising worldwide fear-filled fundamentalist tide seeping into religions everywhere: the embrace of paradox and uncertainty as the virtuoso expression of life-giving humility. Our egos must be curtailed by what we do not know, which is far more than we do know. This humility is rooted in a fact: we are at the beginning of creation and don't have any clue as to how things will grow and change.

To me Carolyn Baker's *Confronting Christofascism: Healing the Evangelical Wound* is a liberating "anti-theology." She speaks about what may *not* be said about God. And this way of perceiving God is found not just in ancient Christianity but in the best of other religions too, or for that matter in the work of people like my friend Dr. Marlene Winell, a psychologist, educator, and writer whom Baker quotes as a groundbreaker in studying the deadly impact of fundamentalist religion on individuals.

Not long ago, wholesale loss of faith and the "inevitable" rise of science-based secularism were predicted. What has actually happened has been a worldwide resurgence of fundamentalist extremism within all religions from the Islamic "brotherhoods" (Taliban, ISIS, etc.) and Hindu nationalism to the North American "religious right" fundamentalism of the MAGA/Trump kind, which (if I may say so) came within a hair of destroying America entirely and is now arrayed against democracy itself. This resurgence of brutal fundamentalism can only herald civil wars across the globe (including the actual violence in the USA that I predicted long ago as these groups turned to White Nationalist terror). Civil wars of (and about) religion are being fought over the control of the hearts and minds of religionists of every faith. This struggle pits tolerant open faith against paranoid reactionary fascist "faith" seeking power over others, by whatever name.

In *Confronting Christofascism*, Carolyn Baker has offered a way out of the looming wars of religion through 1) writing a true history of the USA's fundamentalist/evangelical movement and 2) offering the first steps on a path to freedom for those wishing to reconsider fascist religion and escape. This is an important book.

Frank Schaeffer
author of *Fall in Love, Have Children, Stay Put, Save the Planet, Be Happy*

INTRODUCTION

At this moment American constitutional democracy is sitting on a knife's edge between maintaining a democratic republic or succumbing to the tidal wave of authoritarianism that appears to be engulfing numerous nations globally. Enabling this terrifying trend is the Religious Right in America whose members identify as evangelical or fundamentalist Christians. This movement not only threatens the American republic but has served to traumatize countless numbers of its followers who have joined its ranks in order to make sense of the dizzying changes and daunting challenges of our time. A path to healing and sanity for individuals and the culture is offered in this book.

As investigative reporter Sarah Posner wrote in *Unholy: Why White Evangelicals Worship At The Altar of Donald Trump,* "in Trump, the Christian right sees more than a politician who delivers on promises; they see a savior from the excesses of liberalism."[1] As it was in the earliest days of fundamentalist Christianity in America, no compromise with what it identifies as righteous, no betrayal of its own values , no assault on objective, verifiable reality is too much to ask in order to buttress itself from having to abide with the assumptions and behaviors that it deems threatening to its worldview.

At this writing in 2021, I believe that there is no greater threat to democracy than the burgeoning tide of authoritarianism in the United States and throughout the world. In the wake of climate chaos, massive global economic inequality, systemic racism and ethnocentrism, and the potential collapse of systems and institutions swirling within unprecedented political divergence, democracy is now in critical condition, in fact, almost on life-support.

On January 6, 2021, with the collusion of specific members of the Republican Party, a violent attack was launched on the United States Capitol by supporters of Donald Trump in response to his request to contest and violently overthrow the election of Joe Biden to the Presidency. Apparently, the insurrectionists intended not only to stop the certification of the election by the Electoral College, but to intimidate or even kill the Vice-President and Speaker of the House. In the process five people died, and 140 were severely injured. Whereas the rioting ceased within a few hours, the insurrection did not.

In fact, some leaders of the Republican Party have launched a massive campaign to suppress voting in numerous states and to conduct new election "audits" of votes in the 2020 Presidential election. These efforts constitute an ongoing insurgency movement to undermine the democratic process and the 2024 Presidential election. What is more, the Republican Party has rejected a Congressional vote to investigate the January 6 insurrection, forcing the Speaker of the House to ultimately create a select committee of investigators with subpoena power.

Now, in mid-2021, 53% of Republicans do not believe that Joe Biden is the legitimate President of The United States. Of those, three out of five white evangelicals contest the reality of Biden's victory.[2]

Alongside their doubt of Biden as President, many evangelicals are embracing the conspiracy cult of QAnon, according to a May, 2021 *New York Times* report, "QAnon Now as Popular in U.S. as Some Major Religions, Poll Suggests."[3] Additionally, the *UK Independent* reports that "QAnon has merged with white Christian evangelicals, experts say—and the results could be lethal."[4]

In *How Democracies Die*, Steven Levitsky and Daniel Ziblatt argue that, "This is how democracies now die. Blatant dictatorship—in the form of fascism, communism, or military rule—has disappeared across much of the world. Military coups and other violent seizures of power are rare. Most countries hold regular elections. Democracies still die, but by different means. Since the end of the Cold War, most democratic breakdowns have been caused not by generals and soldiers but by elected governments themselves. Like Chávez in Venezuela, elected leaders have subverted democratic institutions in Georgia, Hungary, Nicaragua, Peru, the Philippines, Poland, Russia, Sri Lanka, Turkey, and Ukraine. Democratic backsliding today begins at the ballot box."[5]

Religious fundamentalism in any form is antithetical to our deepest humanity regardless of the creed by which it is driven.

It is now painfully obvious that democracy in the United States is experiencing death by a thousand cuts, and white evangelicals are massively enabling its demise. I believe that it is essential to trace the historical context in which Christian fundamentalism arose in the nineteenth century in order to understand how this could happen. Even more urgent is the need to examine how fundamentalist Christianity has severely traumatized its followers and explore specific tools for recovering from it, as well as pondering what actions might be taken to prevent the further decimation of American democracy, enabled as it is by evangelical elements of the Republican Party.

I am offering an exploration of these as someone who was born and raised in fundamentalist Christianity and made a dangerous and daunting escape from its isolating and other-worldly existence to join life in the human race.

While technical differences between "fundamentalist" and "evangelical" may be important for some readers, I consider them hairsplitting, and I will be using them interchangeably in this book.

To those who seek to heal the wounds that their engagement with Christian fundamentalism may have created, I offer support and encouragement, noting that within the latter word is the word "courage." The journey of healing from religious trauma requires nothing if not courage, and countless people every day are finding it as they leave the evangelical movement in droves.

Although this book is not primarily a political missive, the political landscape cannot be separated from the religious one, because, since the end of World War II, evangelicals have sought, at the very least, to markedly influence American politics, and at the very worst, to collude with politicians to create a theocracy, or "government by God."

I have written this book from a sense of profound urgency in the context of the mindboggling deterioration of democracy in the United States. The future of the American experiment is more uncertain than it has ever been. Journalist Chauncey DeVega recently interviewed a historian who believes that Joe Biden "may be a speed bump on the fascists' march to power."[6] In other words, we may have a reprieve from the fast-track fascism of the Trump Administration, but from my perspective, awake Americans must actively oppose the anti-democratic policies of the Republican Party and its theocratic enablers of the Religious Right so that we will not succumb, as so many previously democratic nations have, to autocracy. The end product of the collusion between the Religious Right and Trumpian Republicans is what I and others have called Christo-fascism.

The first section of this book will document how this happened, tracing the development of evangelicalism in America from the nineteenth century to the present moment. The evangelical movement and its political involvement cannot be fully understood without a historical context.

The second section begins with my own story of growing up in a fundamentalist Christian home and traces the process of extricating myself from the fundamentalist worldview. In that section I offer to those who are recovering from their fundamentalist experience, or may be struggling with it, options for personal healing and an appreciation of their humanity in an indisputably challenging world. The book concludes with a rigorously honest assessment of what is becoming increasingly difficult to distinguish: the boundaries between evangelical Christianity and the politics of the Republican Party. Finally, I endeavor to inspire the reader to utilize their engagement with fundamentalism in whatever form, to actively move beyond the wounds of that culture toward informed civic responsibility during a global epidemic of authoritarianism.

Climate catastrophe is an existential threat to our species, as is the accompanying collapse of systems resulting from climate change and economic implosion. Yet although these crises are imminent, I believe that a world (including a nation called America) governed largely by authoritarians is a problem requiring immediate attention. No matter how involved with or removed from Christian fundamentalism you are, I urge you to read this book and allow your conscience to compel you to informed, audacious action.

PART I

THE HISTORICAL & CULTURAL CONTEXT

1. UNDERSTANDING CRISTOFASCISM

If the alliance between these zealots and the government succeeds, it will snuff out the last vestiges of American democracy.

—Chris Hedges[1]

Post-Truth is Pre-Fascism.

—Timothy Snyder

How is it that anyone can accurately use the term "Christofascism" to describe the marriage of evangelical Christianity and fascist ideology in the twenty-first century? "Christo" is an adjective meaning Christian, and combining it with the word *fascism* may feel sacrilegious for those who consider the two concepts to be antithetical to one another. Indeed, if Christianity is defined as the summation of the teachings of Christ, the two words cannot be reconciled. If, however, the Christianity in question minimizes the teachings of Christ and maximizes the writings of Christ's apostles, glorifies the fathers of the early Christian church, and interprets all of the Bible literally for the purpose of declaring that humans are inherently sinful, and that accepting Jesus

Christ as their personal savior is the only way their sinful condition can be forgiven, whereas not accepting Jesus as their personal savior consigns them to eternity in hell—in that case, we are dealing with something far beyond the contents of the Christian gospels.

And what specifically is fascism?

Yale historian Jason Stanley writes that "Fascism is not a new threat, but rather a permanent temptation."[2] Stanley argues that fascism generally follows a specific formula:

1. Conjuring a "mythic past" that has supposedly been destroyed ("by liberals, feminists, and immigrants"). These myths rely on an "overwhelming sense of nostalgia for a past that is racially pure, traditional, and patriarchal." Fascist leaders "position themselves as father figures and strongmen" who alone can restore lost greatness. And yes, the fascist leader is "always a 'he.'"

2. Fascist leaders sow division; they succeed by "turning groups against each other," inflaming historical antagonisms and ancient hatreds for their own advantage. Social divisions in themselves—between classes, religions, ethnic groups and so on —are what we might call pre-existing conditions. Fascists may not invent the hate, but they cynically instrumentalize it: demonizing outgroups, normalizing and naturalizing bigotry, stoking violence to justify repressive "law and order" policies, the curtailing of civil rights and due process, and the mass imprisonment and killing of manufactured enemies.

3. Fascists "attack the truth" with propaganda, in particular "a kind of anti-intellectualism" that "creates a petri dish for conspiracy theories." Hannah Arendt, who was a German political theorist living in exile during Hitler's reign, wrote that fascism relies on "a consistent and total substitution of lies for factual truth." She described the phenomenon as destroying "the sense by which we take our bearings in the real world....

[T]he category of truth verses falsehood [being] among the mental means to this end." In such an atmosphere, anything is possible, no matter how previously unthinkable.[3]

In 1939, 20,000 Americans rallied in New York's Madison Square Garden to celebrate the rise of Nazism – an event largely forgotten from American history. American Nazis marched into the hall in the party's brown uniforms, reciting the pledge of allegiance and listening to the national anthem before giving Nazi salutes. Fritz Kuhn, the leader of the German-American Bund (the American wing of the Nazi party), railed against the "Jewish-controlled media" and said it was time to return the United States to the white Christians who he said founded the nation. At one point during the speech a 26-year-old plumber's helper from Brooklyn named Isadore Greenbaum charged the stage and yelled, "Down with Hitler." He was beaten up by Bund guards and his clothing ripped off in the attack before New York police officers arrested him for disorderly conduct. Over the whole scene loomed a giant multistory image of George Washington with Nazi emblems on either side.[4]

In 1939, Kuhn was charged with embezzlement, imprisoned, and stripped of his citizenship. Many of the Bund's assets were seized. Without leadership, the Bund fell apart. Once Nazi Germany began invading other European nations that same year, support for Nazism in the United States diminished even more, and by the time American soldiers were deployed, support for Nazi ideology was taboo. But that doesn't mean support for the type of racism and nationalism supported by the Nazis ever went away, even in the years immediately after World War II.[5] In fact, fascism in the United States had been growing in popularity in the 1920s and '30s, and it may be that its success was drastically tempered only by the Presidency of Franklin Roosevelt.

One of the frustrating realities of our time is that terms like *fascism* and *socialism* are used interchangeably with little understanding of their authentic meaning. Confusion of the terms often results from a general resistance to authoritarianism. But although authoritarianism under fascism and under socialism may look the same, in most cases the motivations are different. Authoritarian socialism as we witnessed under Stalin looked quite different from democratic socialism such as that of Salvador Allende of Chile or Bernie Sanders in the United States. However, in the current political milieu in the United States, many people who do not understand the political motivations behind different forms of authoritarianism accuse the political left of being "socialist," which for them is synonymous with authoritarianism. At the same time, they do not grasp that the "freedom" promised to them by the Trump Administration is, in fact, a twenty-first-century version of fascism.

CHARACTERISTICS OF FASCISM

In 1995, Umberto Eco, the late Italian intellectual giant and novelist most famous for *The Name of the Rose*, wrote a guide describing the primary features of fascism. As a child, Eco was a loyalist of Mussolini, an experience that made him quick to detect the markers of fascism later in life, when he became a revered public intellectual and political voice. Eco made the essential point, which we need to remember, that *fascism looks different in each incarnation, morphing with time and leadership, as "it would be difficult for [it] to reappear in the same form in different historical circumstances."*[6]

In her 2016 Alternet article, "Trump Is an Eerily Perfect Match with a Famous 14-Point Guide to Identify Fascist Leaders," Kali Holloway summarizes the ways in which Donald Trump conforms to Eco's 14-point guide:

1. *The Cult of Tradition:* Let's make America great again. Holloway asks, "Remind me when America was great, again? Was it during the eras of native people genocide, slavery, black lynchings as white entertainment, Japanese-American internment, or Jim Crow?"

2. *Rejection of Modernism:* Trump denies climate change and supports fracking and opposes environmental regulations that protect the land and people from its devastations. He favors cuts to NASA and critical biomedical research. Likewise, evangelical former Vice President, Mike Pence, is a fervent denier of science and is a religious zealot. Pence has written that global warming is a "myth," that the earth is cooling, and that there is "growing skepticism" among scientists about climate change—all literally the opposite of the truth.

3. *The Cult of Action for Action's Sake:* For example, as Holloway notes, "Anti-intellectualism and pride in idiocy—and disdain for complexity—are trademarks of today's Republican ideology. In this light, educated elites are the enemies of salt-of-the-earth, hard-working (white) Americans. Their hatred of Obama was paired with disdain for what they view as his 'effete snob[bery]' and proclivity for lattes and arugula." In addition, "He [Trump] told the *Washington Post* he has 'never' read much because he makes decisions based on 'very little knowledge . . . because I have a lot of common sense.' After winning the election, Trump waived the daily intelligence briefings that far better-prepared and knowledgeable predecessors made time for, despite his being the first president with no experience in government or the military."

4. ***Opposition to Analytical Criticism; Disagreement Is Treason:*** According to Holloway, "Trump attempts to quell the slightest criticism or dissent with vitriol and calls for violence. On the campaign trail, Trump encouraged his base's mob mentality, promising to 'pay for the legal fees' if they would 'knock the crap' out of protesters. He gushed about 'the old days' when protesters would be 'carried out on a stretcher.' When the media finally began taking a critical tone after giving him billions in criticism-free press, Trump declared his real opponent was the 'crooked press.' He pettily stripped reporters of press credentials when they wrote something he didn't like, referred to individual reporters as 'scum,' 'slime,' 'dishonest' and 'disgusting,' and claimed he would 'open up' libel laws so he could sue over unfavorable—though not erroneous—coverage. In the latter stages of the campaign, Trump supporters took to berating the media with shouts of 'lügenpresse,' a German phrase popular with Nazis that translates as 'lying press.' Some Trump supporters also sported T-shirts suggesting journalists should be lynched."

5. ***Exploiting and Exacerbating the Natural Fear of Difference:*** "The first appeal of a fascist or prematurely fascist movement is an appeal against the intruders." Explaining how this plays out in Trump's world, Holloway writes that "before he officially threw his hat into the ring, Trump courted bigots and racists furious about Obama's wins by pushing the birther lie and attempting to delegitimize the first black president. The only coherent policy proposals Trump made during his run were those that appealed to white racial resentments, promising to end Muslim immigration, build a wall along the southern border

to keep Mexicans out, and retweeting white nationalists' made-up statistics about black criminality."

6. *Appeal to Frustrated Middle Classes:* "Eco writes that fascism reaches out to 'a class suffering from an economic crisis or feelings of political humiliation, and frightened by the pressure of lower social groups.'" Clearly, Holloway argues, "Trump made overt appeals to whites who believe the American Dream is not so much slipping from their grasp as being snatched away by undeserving immigrants and other perceived outsiders. Trump made impossible promises to return manufacturing jobs and restore class and social mobility to a group of people nervous about falling down rungs on the ladder."

7. *Obsession with a Plot, Possibly an International One:* Holloway writes that "Trump obviously appealed to racial and religious nationalist sentiments among a majority of white Americans by scapegoating Mexican and Muslim immigrants on issues of crime, job losses and terrorism. He pushed the idea that he would 'put America first,' suggesting that Hillary Clinton would favor other nations over the U.S." Unquestionably, Trump used this tactic with his supporters to scapegoat people of color, foreigners, and President Obama as responsible for the suffering of white working and middle-class Americans.

8. *Followers Must Feel Humiliated by the Ostentatious Wealth and Force of Their Enemies:* Holloway aptly summarizes this: "Trump conjured up a vision of America in a downward spiral, a nation fallen from its lofty position in the world to one deserving of shame and ridicule. He spent much of the campaign telling Americans they weren't just losing, but had become

the butt of an embarrassing worldwide joke."
Throughout the campaign, Trump hammered home
the notion that our enemies are laughing at us and
that we have been made the laughing stock of the
world.

9. ***Pacifism Is Trafficking with the Enemy. It's Bad
Because Life Is Permanent Warfare:*** Holloway points
out that "Trump has made expansion of the U.S.
military a primary aim, putting the country in a
perpetually defensive stance. In the past, he has
reportedly demanded to know why the U.S. shouldn't
use its nuclear weapons. In the weeks after his
election, he filled his cabinet with war hawks. On the
campaign trail, Trump said his generals would have
30 days following his election to put together 'a plan
for soundly and quickly defeating ISIS.'

10. ***Popular Elitism:*** Astutely, Holloway grasps one of the
principal lynchpins of the Trump world view.
"Trump repeatedly hails himself as the best. He has
the best words, the best ideas, the best campaign, the
best gold-plated penthouse, the best of all the best of
the best things. Trump and his nationalist followers
believe that America is the greatest country that has
ever existed. That somehow makes Americans the
best people on Earth, by dint of birth. In keeping
with a long-standing right-wing lie about patriotism
and love of country, conservatives are the best
Americans, and Trump supporters are the best of all."
As Holloway reminds us, "Trump biographer
Michael D'Antonio wrote that Trump's father
instilled in his son that 'most people are weaklings,'
and thus don't deserve respect. Trump, who earned a
reputation as a lifelong bully in both his public and
private lives, has consistently bemoaned America's

weakness, resulting from the reign of weak cultural elites."

11. *Everybody Is Educated to Become a Hero:* "Trump's base believes itself to be the last of a dying (white) breed of American heroes," says Holloway, "enduring multiculturalism and political correctness to speak truth to the powerful elites and invading hordes of outsiders who have marginalized and oppressed them, or taken what's rightfully theirs. Eco writes that "this cult of heroism is strictly linked with the cult of death.

12. *Transfer of Will to Power in Sexual Matters:* We've heard it all so many times, but Holloway reminds us again that "we are well acquainted with Trump's machismo, which, like all machismo, is inseparable from his loudly broadcast misogyny. This is a man who defended the size of his penis in the middle of a nationally televised political debate. For 30 years, including the 18 months of his campaign, Trump has consistently reduced women to their looks or what he deems the desirability of their bodies, including when talking about his own daughter, whom he constantly reminds us he would be dating if not for incest laws. Trump has been particularly vicious to women in the media, tweeting insults their way, suggesting they're having their periods when they ask questions he doesn't like, and verbally attacking them at rallies and inviting his supporters to follow suit. There's also that notorious, leaked 2005 recording of Trump discussing grabbing women by the genitalia, which was followed by a stream of women accusing him of sexual assault."

13. *Selective Populism:* "Since no large quantity of human beings can have a common will," Eco writes, "the

Leader pretends to be their interpreter. . . ." Holloway elaborates: "There is in our future a TV or internet populism, in which the emotional response of a selected group of citizens can be presented and accepted as the Voice of the People. Eco's two-decade-old prediction is uncanny. Trump, a fixture on social media and reality television, has mastered a kind of TV and internet populism that makes his voice one with the angry masses of his base. At the Republican National Convention, after a rant about the terrible, dystopian shape of the country, he designated himself the nation's sole savior. 'I am your voice,' Trump said. 'No one knows the system better than me. Which is why I alone can fix it.'" Holloway asks, "Is there any more vivid example of Eco's example than Trump's repeated contention that the election was rigged? Trump painted himself as the savior of a people who could no longer rely on rich, powerful politicians. Save for him, of course."

14. *The Use of Newspeak:* *Newspeak* is the fictional language in the dystopian novel 1984, by George Orwell. "All the Nazi or Fascist schoolbooks made use of an impoverished vocabulary, and an elementary syntax, in order to limit the instruments for complex and critical reasoning," Eco writes. "But we must be ready to identify other kinds of *Newspeak*, even if they take the apparently innocent form of a popular talk show." Summarizing, Holloway notes, "Trump also kept his sentences short and his words to as few syllables as possible. He repeated words he wanted to drive home, and punctuated his speech with phrases meant to have maximum effect. In lots of cases, a single quote contained multiple contradictory statements. The takeaway from a Trump speech was

whatever the listener wanted to hear, which turned out to be a winning strategy."

In his 2018 Literary Hub article, "Fascism is Not an Idea to Be Debated, It's a Set of Actions to Fight," author and survivor of the Balkan Wars of the 1990s, Aleksandar Hemon, writing about Trump advisor Steve Bannon, says:

> If Bannon were to be called as he is, a fascist, the marketplace of ideas would have to confront the fact that the American government is being rapidly radicalized, that things unimaginable might be around the corner, and that there are many tempting paths to full collaboration... It is frightening to think we could be entering the civil war mode, wherein none of the differences and disagreements can be hashed out in discussion. It is quite possible that there is no resolution to the present situation until one side is thoroughly destroyed as an ideological power and political entity. If that is the case, the inescapable struggle requires that anti-fascist forces clearly identify the enemy and commit to defeating them, whoever they are, whatever it takes. The time of conversations with fascists is over, even if they might be your best friend from high school.[7]

Author and radio host Thom Hartmann wrote in his article, "America is at a fascist turning point—and only totally disempowering and humiliating Trump will stop it":

> The main key to fascism, the one element that shows up in fascist takeovers worldwide and has for a century, is the emergence of a strongman leader who uses age-old aspects of toxic masculinity to draw in and hold his mostly-male followers...The attraction to the strongman comes from his projection of masculinity, which draws authoritarian follower-

types like a magnet, usually demonstrated by his willingness to break laws and norms in the service of his power and his claimed (and usually simplistic) 'solutions to the problems of society.' Misogyny is also always featured in fascistic authoritarian regimes."[8]

The attack on the Capitol of the United States on January 6, 2021 by insurrectionists seeking to overturn the election of Joe Biden as President, viciously seeking to hang then Vice President Mike Pence and to kill Speaker of the House Nancy Pelosi, was carried out by a fascist mob, even if the members of that mob did not openly identify as fascists.

In addition to the January 6 insurrection, Republican members of Congress have openly disavowed the Constitution of the United States and the American experiment itself. History Professor Robert McElvaine writes, "Put more plainly, it is the Trump acolytes and members of the Republican Party who have joined in their leader's efforts to overthrow the American republic who are Republicans in Name Only.... their efforts to define themselves as conservatives is little more than a falsehood. Actual conservatives value responsibility, self-reliance, tradition, norms, law, truth-telling, morality, manners, knowledge, loyalty, success in business, self-control, religious values, patriotism, stability, maturity, marital fidelity, a sense of history, the checks and balances of constitutional government, deliberation, fiscal restraint, accountability, ordered liberty, justice, principle, humility and compassion."[9]

Many Republicans say that they no longer trust elections. In fact, they admit that if they don't keep people from voting, they will lose elections, and they seem willing to take power by whatever means necessary.[10] Thus, at this writing, we are witnessing massive efforts by the Republican Party, through a variety of tactics, to suppress voting by people of color and those likely to vote for Democrats. Whereas during the four years of the Trump Administration, many non-Republicans believed that the GOP's loyalty to Trump was based on fear of his political power over them, it has now become tragically obvious that their loyalty is not based on fear, but on the fact that they are in alignment with his authoritarian worldview. They no longer believe in rule by the people, but rule by oligarchy and white supremacy. These two components, bolstered by an authoritarian leader, are the essential ingredients of political and cultural fascism.

WHITE EVANGELICALS AND FASCISM

In 1970, German liberation theologian and activist Dorothy Sölle coined the term *Christofascism,* which means the intersection between fascism and Christianity. It also encompasses the fascistic, totalitarian, and imperialistic aspects of the Christian church. German-American philosopher and theologian Paul Tillich stated that American Christian fundamentalism has turned Christ into something that is "dictatorial in its heart and is preparing society for an American fascism." It has "allowed Christians to impose themselves not only upon other religions but other cultures and political parties which do not go under the banner of the final, normative, victorious Christ" [11]

Evangelical Christianity is by definition imperialistic because it believes one of its primary responsibilities is to "evangelize," or preach the Christian gospel for the purpose of converting others to it.

The terms evangelical and fundamentalist are often used interchangeably, which is not technically accurate. Both feel compelled to preach the gospel and convert, but fundamentalist Christians without exception interpret the Bible literally, whereas there is a slight difference of opinion among evangelicals regarding Biblical interpretation . Nevertheless, in this book, I am using the terms interchangeably.

Insofar as any worldview feels compelled to proselytize

15

others, Christian fundamentalism is, in my opinion, imperialistic, and as I will demonstrate, many American evangelicals have played an essential and blatant role in the development of Christofascism in recent years.

In *The Evangelicals: The Struggle To Shape America*, Frances Fitzgerald defines evangelical as: "...reliance on the Bible as the ultimate religious authority; *crucicentrism*, or a focus on Christ's redemption of mankind on the cross; *conversionism*, or the emphasis on a 'new birth' as a life-changing experience; and activism, or concern with sharing the faith with others."[12]

It is worth noting that although Christians have evangelized since the very beginning of the religion, fundamentalist Christianity is a more modern phenomenon with more opportunities to evangelize and to manipulate individuals and cultures in the direction of conversion and devotion to the faith. Fundamentalism began as a movement in American Protestantism in the late 19th century in reaction to theological modernism, which aimed to revise traditional Christian beliefs to accommodate new developments in the natural and social sciences, especially the theory of biological evolution. Fundamentalist Christians are fiercely attached to maintaining the "fundamentals" of historic Christianity and rigorously opposed to updating or modernizing it. Christian theological modernism often based its updated perspective on new interpretations of the Bible which were not literal, and that was anathema to the fundamentalist movement.

LITERAL INTERPRETATION OF THE BIBLE

The lifeblood of fundamentalist Christianity is the literal interpretation of the Bible. Biblical literalists believe that, unless a passage is clearly intended by the writer as allegory, poetry, or some other genre, the Bible should be interpreted as literal statements by the author.[13] This approach to scripture is used extensively by fundamentalists, in contrast to the historical-critical method used by mainstream Judaism or mainline Protestantism.[14]

Therefore, when Genesis states that the Earth was created in seven days, fundamentalists believe that it was actually created in seven *literal* days. In the Genesis account of the Great Flood, fundamentalists believe that not only did the Great Flood occur, but that Noah literally built an ark and took into the ark two of every kind of animal that existed on Earth at that time.

Problems occur for fundamentalists when literal interpretation clashes with the metaphorical. For example, the often-quoted words of Jesus to Nicodemus in John, Chapter Three, "Ye must be born again," cannot be interpreted literally. Nicodemus actually asks Jesus, "Can a man enter the second time into his mother's womb?" In this passage, the literal interpretation would be absurd, so fundamentalists have conveniently referred to "Ye must be born again" as a metaphor. They further construed Jesus' metaphorical words to mean that every human being must accept Jesus as their personal savior; otherwise, they will not be born again, which means they will not be able to enter heaven when they die and will be sent to hell by God.

Christian fundamentalism also teaches that the Bible is inerrant, meaning that every word is true and that it is free of errors because it is "divinely inspired." Accordingly, each book of the Bible was revealed by God, meaning that every word and its meaning was dictated by God to the writer.

Given the historical criticism of the Bible that has evolved over millennia, its overwhelmingly literal interpretation is all but non-existent, except among evangelical and fundamentalist Christians. American New Testament scholar and former fundamentalist Bart Ehrman writes in *Misquoting Jesus*:

How do these millions of people know what is in the New Testament? They "know" because scholars with unknown names, identities, backgrounds, qualifications, predilections, theologies, and personal opinions have told them what is in the New Testament. But what if the translators have translated the wrong text? It has happened before. The King James Version is filled with places in which the translators rendered a Greek text derived ultimately from Erasmus's edition, which was based on a single twelfth-century manuscript that is one of the worst of the manuscripts that we now have available to us! It's no wonder that modern translations often differ from the King James, and no wonder that some Bible-believing Christians prefer to pretend there's never been a problem, since God inspired the King James Bible instead of the original Greek! (As the old song goes, "If the King James was good enough for Saint Paul, it's good enough for me.")

Reality is never that neat, however, and in this case we need to face up to the facts. The King James was not given by God, but was a translation by a group of scholars in the early seventeenth century who based their rendition on a faulty Greek text. Later, translators based their translations on Greek texts that were better, but not perfect. Even the translation you hold in your hands is affected by these textual problems we have been discussing, whether you are a reader of the New International Version, the Revised Standard Version, the New Revised Standard Version, the New American Standard Version, the New King James, the Jerusalem Bible, the Good News Bible, or something else. They are all based on texts that have been changed in places. And there are some places in which modern translations continue to transmit what is probably not the original text...Whatever else we may say about the Christian scribes—whether of the early centuries or of the Middle Ages—we have to admit that in addition to copying scripture, they were changing scripture. Sometimes they didn't mean to—they were simply tired, or inattentive, or, on occasion, inept. At other times, though, they did mean to make changes, as when they wanted the text to emphasize precisely what they themselves believed, for example about the nature of Christ, or about the role of women in the church, or about the wicked character of their Jewish opponents.[15]

American progressive Lutheran theologian Marcus Borg writes in *Reading The Bible Again For The First Time*, that:

I let go of the notion that the Bible is a divine product. I learned that it is a human cultural product, the product of two ancient communities, biblical Israel and early Christianity. As such, it contained their understandings and affirmations, not statements coming directly or somewhat directly from God. . . I realized that whatever "divine revelation" and the "inspiration of the Bible" meant (if they meant anything), they did not mean that the Bible was a divine product with divine authority.[16]

Bart Ehrman and Marcus Borg are today viewed as "false teachers" by Christian fundamentalists because, among other things, both question the literal interpretation of the Bible. Of course, Ehrman and Borg are not the only ones to abandon the literal interpretation, but anyone who does so is considered a false teacher in fundamentalist circles.

THE BIRTH OF CHRISTIAN FUNDAMENTALISM

In his *New York Times* article, "The Day Christian Fundamentalism Was Born," Matthew Avery Sutton notes that:

Beginning on May 25, 1919, 6,000 ministers, theologians and evangelists came together in Philadelphia for a weeklong series of meetings. They heard sermons on everything from "Christ and the Present Crisis" to "Why I Preach the Second Coming." The men and women assembled there believed that God had chosen them to call Christians back to the "fundamentals" of the faith, and to prepare the world for one final revival before Jesus returned to earth. They called their group the World's Christian Fundamentals Association.

A Minneapolis Baptist preacher named William Bell Riley organized the meetings. A tall, austere and uncompromising man, Riley was a natural-born crusader, who rarely saw a religious fight he did not think he could win. Under his leadership, the event drew participants from all around the county. Contrary to popular stereotypes, the centers of fundamentalism were in the nation's major northern and western cities—New York, Chicago, Denver, Los Angeles, Seattle—and not the rural South.

The men and women at the conference were all white. On questions of race, fundamentalists defended the status quo. African-American and Latino Christians, even when they shared the same theology as their white counterparts, were systematically excluded from fundamentalist churches and organizations.

In many ways, the Philadelphia meeting marked the public beginning of the new fundamentalist movement. "The hour has struck," Riley declared at the time, "for the rise of a new Protestantism." He described the inauguration of his organization and the rise of fundamentalism as more significant than Martin Luther's posting of the 95 Theses on the church door in Wittenberg, Germany 400 years earlier.[17]

Sutton's article continues to explain the cultural shift that was occurring at this moment. World War I had ended just a few months earlier. American culture was profoundly impacted by "The Great War" as well as numerous advances in learning. The fundamentalist movement became an unprecedented reaction to all things "modern"—modern theology, modern technology, modern science, and modern morals. It also emerged as a very white movement, the Civil War having ended only 54 years earlier. The violent racism and white supremacy that erupted in the Civil War has never been healed and was even more raw and unhealed in 1919. Moreover, the following decade would witness the largest membership in the Ku Klux Klan in the United States in the country's history.

A fundamentalist reaction that would have repercussions well into the twenty-first century was its distrust of science. This skepticism was particularly galvanized in the Scopes Trial, an American legal case in July, 1925 in which a high school teacher, John T. Scopes, was accused of violating Tennessee's Butler Act, which had made it unlawful to teach human evolution in any state-funded school. Today, we are witnessing vehement pushback against science in terms of climate change and resistance among some fundamentalists to receiving the vaccination against Coronavirus. Christian fundamentalism has always viewed science with skepticism because it believes that science is attempting to undermine the Bible and turn the world against Biblical teachings.

The fundamentalist movement which began to congeal in 1919 launched a host of publications, conferences, Bible institutes, and church-run radio stations. At the same time, agonizing divisions in major Protestant denominations resulted from the theological conflagration between fundamentalists and modernists.

The onslaught of social and cultural change catapulted many fundamentalists into pre-occupation with the end times and Biblical prophecy. Surely the apocalypse was just around the corner. As Sutton writes:

> The political positions embraced by early fundamentalists, all
> of which flowed logically from their apocalyptic understanding

of the biblical text, hardened over time. They called for limited government and battled anything that seemed to threaten Christians' rights and freedoms. They fretted about changes in the culture, and especially those that upended what they saw as traditional gender roles. In foreign policy, they championed isolationism and, when they did want the United States to intervene around the world, they called on American leaders to act unilaterally. They also became some of the country's most ardent and unapologetic Zionists.[18]

DARBY AND DISPENSATIONALISM

In the 1830s and '40s, an Irish minister and Bible teacher, John Nelson Darby, traveled to America, where he widely taught the theology of *dispensationalism*, which is a system of biblical interpretation based on the belief that God divided history into dispensations, or defined periods in which God's plan is administered in certain ways. Accordingly, humanity is held responsible as a steward of God's plan during every dispensation. In 1909, an American theologian, pastor, and veteran of the Confederacy, Cyrus Scofield, devised a study Bible based on dispensationalism which became wildly popular among fundamentalists and remains a mainstay among many fundamentalists to this day. Much of American fundamentalism bases its Biblical interpretation on the Scofield Bible, and in fact, Scofield founded Dallas Theological Seminary, which ultimately became the Yale of American fundamentalist theology.

It is crucial to understand that prior to Darby, evangelicals were not as preoccupied with Biblical prophecy or apocalyptic teachings as they are today. Until the rise of the fundamentalist movement, Protestant Christians throughout the world adhered to the traditional teachings of their denominations and generally adapted to progress in the modern world. It seems that World War I, however, attended by a host of rapid changes in science, technology, and morals alongside deepening racism, women's suffrage, and the reality of world war, proved psychologically overwhelming for a host of conventional Christians. Their response was one of reaction, evangelistic zeal, apocalyptic thinking, and religious authoritarianism. Becoming terrified of the transformation of their secular world, they steadily followed a trajectory of passionate proselytization that eventually morphed into twenty-first-century cult-like religious terrorism.

CHRISTIANITY'S SHADOW SIDE

One of the greatest gifts of psychologist Carl Jung was the concept of the shadow. According to Jung, we disown parts of ourselves that are not acceptable to others or to ourselves. Whereas we hope for "out of sight, out of mind," the parts we disown do not disappear. Instead, they live in the unconscious mind, where they eventually erupt in some unexpected fashion, or they drive us to behave in ways that we and others find unacceptable. Jung believed that not only do individuals develop a shadow side, but so do groups, organizations, religions, cultures, governments, and institutions. Everyone and everything has its shadow.

From my perspective, Christianity developed its shadow early on with its gradual departure from the example and teachings of Jesus, constructing layer upon layer of shadow material that eventually came to resemble the very enemies of its existence. Not all Christians or Christian groups acted out the shadow. Many remained true to the example of their founder, but many more did not. Originally, Christianity was persecuted by an empire, then itself became an empire that forced masses of human beings to convert to its religion by force or by coercion.

Fundamentalism is one of many manifestations of Christianity's shadow. Jung wrote that, "The shadow is a moral problem that challenges the whole ego-personality, for no one can become conscious of the shadow without considerable moral effort. To become conscious of it involves recognizing the dark aspects of the personality as present and real. This act is the essential condition for any kind of self-knowledge."[19] While Jung is speaking about the individual, the same applies to institutions. It is the Christian shadow, then, that fundamentalism shamelessly embodies.

THE SEEDS OF CHRISTO-FASCISM

The fundamentalist movement congealed out of "terror" of the modern world, and one of the tragic realities of trauma is that often when people are terrified, they terrorize others. The increasing preoccupation with prophecy and the end times that proliferated in the fundamentalist movement motivated its adherents to zealously attempt to convert non-believers so that "the unsaved" would be "spared" spending eternity in hell, which fundamentalists fervently believed was the inevitable destiny of those who did not experience being "born again."

It is not difficult to conclude that the terror that motivated the fundamentalists of the early twentieth century morphed into the terror-*ism* of the twenty-first century that compelled them to impose their theology on other individuals and on the culture at large in an attempt to evangelize and to dominate what they perceived as a sinful and heretical culture. Since its inception, American fundamentalism has proclaimed that it is not a political movement and that converting people to evangelical Christianity and teaching them how to evangelize others was its single, innocuous mission. However, its covert mission had always been and continues to be the evangelizing of the culture to advance the principles of theocracy or government by a Christian God. With the inauguration of Ronald Reagan, the theocratic intentions of American fundamentalism rapidly became more overt as the political dominance of Republican conservatism swept the nation.

Traditional nonfundamentalist Protestant denominations in the late-nineteenth century confronted cultural upheaval and social change by preaching what became known as the "social gospel" which emphasized the teachings of Jesus in the Beatitudes, such as compassion, alleviating poverty, and unconditional acceptance of the individual regardless of their religion or lack thereof. Fundamentalists rejected the social gospel, emphasizing not so much the teachings of Jesus around mercy and compassion, but rather proclaiming Jesus as the son of God whom each individual must accept as their "personal savior." Fixating on Jesus' declaration to Nicodemus in John, Chapter 3 that "you must be born again," the new-birth, born-again experience now became the focal point of Christian evangelism. For fundamentalist theologians and clergy, the social gospel was irrelevant, even a distraction from what they believed was the principle mission of Christianity: to convert the individual and the culture.

While I have noted the impact of cultural upheaval on the birth of fundamentalism, I believe it is crucial to notice three other aspects of that upheaval that most ignited fundamentalist fervor in the late-nineteenth century and that inflames the rhetoric and behavior of the Religious Right in the twenty-first century. Unless we comprehend the racism, the misogyny, and the economic injustice inherent in American fundamentalism, we will miss the psychological and political factors that have given birth to Christofascism.

2. RACE, GENDER, AND THE PROSPERITY GOSPEL

I am filled with unutterable loathing when I contemplate the religious pomp and show, together with the horrible inconsistencies, which everywhere surround me.
—Frederick Douglass[1]

Wives, submit to your husbands as to the Lord.
—Ephesians 5:22, King James Version (KJV)

If I want to believe God for a $65 million plane, you cannot stop me. You cannot stop me from dreaming. I'm gonna dream until Jesus comes.
—Rev. Creflo Dollar[2]

Frances Fitzgerald notes in *The Evangelicals* that before, during, and after the Civil War, "religion was seen primarily as a matter of the individual's relationship to God and to Christ as a personal savior... Paradoxically, this intensely individualistic, asocial religion created an extraordinary degree of social cohesion among white southerners."[3] However, before the birth of the fundamentalist movement, Protestant Christianity was about practicing the tenets of the church and professing to be a Christian.

The rejection of the social gospel by fundamentalism—a rejection that minimized the social justice teachings of Jesus—was at the same time a determination to assure that the central tenet of Christian fundamentalism would be the new birth. As we will see, fixating on the born-again experience allowed evangelicals to cozy up with myriad forms of racism.

BORN AGAIN WHITE SUPREMACY

Anthea Butler, African-American Professor of Religion at the University of Pennsylvania, notes that evangelical racism, propelled by the benefits of whiteness, has, since the nation's founding, played a provocative role in severely fracturing the electorate. During the buildup to the Civil War, white evangelicals used scripture to defend slavery and nurture the Confederacy. During Reconstruction, they used it to deny the vote to newly emancipated blacks. In the twentieth century, they sided with segregationists in avidly opposing movements for racial equality and civil rights. Most recently, evangelicals supported the Tea Party, a Muslim ban, and border policies allowing family separation. White evangelicals today, cloaked in a vision of Christian patriarchy and nationhood, form a staunch voting bloc in support of white leadership. Evangelicalism's racial history festers, splits America, and needs a reckoning now.[4]

In *White Too Long: The Legacy of White Supremacy In American Christianity*, Southern Baptist minister and professor, Robert P. Jones, traces white supremacy in the Christian church after the Civil War and beyond, and states that "While the South lost the war, this secessionist religion not only survived but also thrived." Having grown up in a Baptist church in Georgia, Jones witnessed the thriving of the secessionist religion firsthand and urgently confronts white Christians accordingly:

It is time—indeed, well beyond time—for white Christians in the United States to reckon with the racism of our past and the willful amnesia of our present. Underneath the glossy, self-congratulatory histories that white Christian churches have written about themselves is a thinly veiled, deeply troubling reality. White Christian churches have not just been complacent; they have not only been complicit; rather, as the dominant cultural power in America, they have been responsible for constructing and sustaining a project to protect white supremacy and resist black equality. This project has framed the entire American story.[5]

While many white Protestant churches of the twenty-first century have become more inclusive and diverse, Christian fundamentalism in America is a predominantly white movement. It has been shaped by white supremacy, and it shamelessly perpetuates it.

As the Fitzgerald quote above reminds us, post-Civil War fundamentalism became increasingly individualistic, especially as it disavowed the social gospel. What mattered now was not racism or social injustice, but whether one has had the new birth experience.

Not only has white supremacy remained and even grown more deeply entrenched in the Christian church since the Civil War, but white supremacy itself has influenced Christian, particularly fundamentalist Christian theology. Regarding this influence, Jones asks:

What if the racist views of historical "titans of the faith" infected the entire theological project contemporary white Christians have inherited from top to bottom? If white supremacy was an unquestionable cultural assumption in America, what does it mean that Christian doctrines by necessity had to develop in ways that were compatible with that worldview? What if, for example, Christian conceptions of marriage and family, the doctrine of biblical inerrancy, or even the concept of having a personal relationship with Jesus developed as they did because they were useful tools for reinforcing white dominance? Is it possible that the white supremacy heresy is so integrated into white Christian DNA that it eludes even sincere efforts to excise it? White Christianity has been many things for America. But whatever else it has been—and the country is indebted to it for a good many things—it has also been the primary institution legitimizing and propagating white power and dominance. Is such a system, built and maintained not just to save souls but also to secure white supremacy, flawed beyond redemption? If we're even going to begin to answer these questions, we need to take a deeper dive into the inner logic of white Christian theology.[6]

As noted above, before the Civil War and World War I, Protestant Christians were far less pre-occupied with "end times." For many Southern Christians, the Confederacy was a signal that God's ideal for human society was being realized. The stunning and humiliating loss by the South diminished this optimism and catapulted many white Christians into a more pessimistic view of God's plan. It was in this exact context that Cyrus Scofield, a Confederate war veteran from Tennessee, published his reference Bible. Thus, we must ask: To what extent was fundamentalist Christian theology influenced by the Confederate sensibilities of Scofield, and given that he founded an entire theological seminary which thousands of evangelicals have attended subsequently, what elements of systemic racism have informed the theology and ethics of the fundamentalist movement overall?

Commenting on the end times obsession, Jones states that, "The most significant outcome of this shift is that the logic of premillennial theology [the belief in the physical return of Jesus in the end times] undercuts calls to social justice, since it proceeds from the presumption that the world is evil and in continual decline. The presence of injustice is the unsurprising outcome of a fallen world, not a call for action. Major human intervention is futile, since the world is beyond anything but divine redemption. *In due time, Christ will return and set things right. In the meantime, rather than reforming the world, Christians should focus on spirituality and the care of souls: deeper Christian discipleship for themselves and salvation for others who are not "saved."*[7] [Emphasis mine]

RACISM IS THE BACKBONE OF THE RELIGIOUS RIGHT

Many analysts of the Religious Right in the 1980s have opined that it grew out of opposition to abortion and the *Roe v. Wade* Supreme Court ruling. Confronting this assumption, Dartmouth College Professor Randall Balmer asserts that "although abortion had emerged as a rallying cry by 1980, the real roots of the Religious Right lie not in the defense of a fetus but in the defense of racial segregation."[8]

In an interview with Anthea Butler, she draws lines from Biblical references used in defense of slavery through Reconstruction when Black men were framed as a sexual menace against virtuous white women, and evangelical believers and churches engaged in lynching. And today, commenting on the recent murder of Asian women at an Atlanta massage parlor, Butler states, "…evangelicalism has been wrapped up in Christian nationalism and these ideas about morality that have been detrimental to the country. I mean, we can see that in the recent murder of six Asian women and the two unfortunate people who happened to be there. There's a guy that kills eight people because he has a pornography addiction, but yet still he's born again and saved and in a Baptist church that preached against all that kind of stuff. And then we have a sheriff who tells us that shooting several Asian women in a massage parlor wasn't "racially motivated."[9]

Social responsibility and care for one's neighbor was increasingly thrown out with the bathwater, and to this day, it is incomprehensible to countless human beings outside of fundamentalist Christianity that fundamentalists care so much about everyone else's "personal relationship with Jesus Christ," and so little about their human needs. Or as Jones writes, "It's nothing short of astonishing that a religious tradition with this relentless emphasis on salvation and one so hyper-attuned to personal sin can simultaneously maintain such blindness to social sins swirling about it, such as slavery and race-based segregation and bigotry."[10]

What is more, many depictions of Jesus by white evangelicals have resulted in a "white Jesus" who hardly looks like a poor, disheveled carpenter from Nazareth. Jones asserts that, "in the white evangelical conception of Jesus, though not often interrogated, Jesus is white, or, as in the late nineteenth-century racial classifications, an Aryan Caucasian. There are no descriptions of Jesus's physical characteristics in the gospels, and what we do know—that he was Jewish and from the Middle East— easily makes nonsense of any claims that Jesus shared with white American Christians a European heritage. But from the white European point of view, shot through with colonialist assumptions about racial hierarchies and white supremacy, there was no other possible conclusion. The story of human salvation had to find expression in a divinely ordained, hierarchical universe. As the exemplar of what it meant to be perfectly human, Jesus by definition had to be white. Whites simply couldn't conceive of owing their salvation to a representative of what they considered an inferior race. And a nonwhite Jesus would render impossible the intimate relationalism necessary

31

for the evangelical paradigm to function: no proper white Christian would let a brown man come into their hearts or submit themselves to be a disciple of a swarthy Semite."[11]

During the 1960s it was stunning to witness white Christians who were appalled by long-haired, sandal-wearing hippies who more closely resembled the historical Jesus than white America's depictions of a European-looking Jesus in evangelical literature and art. Even now in the twenty-first century, many evangelicals assume that godliness is synonymous with short-haired, buttoned-down whiteness.

MASTERS OF MISOGYNY

Religions of the "book," sometimes known as Abrahamic religions—Islam, Judaism, and Christianity—are inherently misogynistic. Their scriptures were penned by men in cultures where women had no place except the bedroom or the kitchen. Every woman I have known who grew up in Christian fundamentalism felt that females were irrelevant in a milieu of male domination. The irrelevance of women was not to be questioned, and prior to the women's movement, rarely was. God was male, Jesus was male, the disciples were male, and until the twentieth century, pastors, deacons, and church officials were predominantly male.

Not only were women irrelevant, but they were suspect. Created from the rib of Adam and usually portrayed in the Bible as seductive, conniving, or mindless martyrs, men were the protagonists and heroes, and women were "supporting actresses" in the ongoing saga of male superiority. Whereas many women in the early Christian church were highly regarded and were active as teachers and pastors, they were not allowed to perform religious instruction or administer sacraments. During this time Christianity became firmly rooted in Greek and Roman culture in terms of gender roles.

The writings of Paul in the New Testament were blatantly sexist. Essentially, they pointed to the innate inferiority of women and implied that the higher intellect belongs to men and the lower intellect belongs to women. The writings of Tertullian, Origen, Augustine, Jerome, Clement of Alexandria, Chrysostom, and other church fathers reveal a misogynist mentality that perceived women as daughters of Eve who were mentally and spiritually inferior to males. Even before conception, women were inferior. They do not have, nor should they have, control over their own bodies.

Dr. Hannelie Wood, Professor of Philosophy and Theology at the University of South Africa, in *Feminists and their perspectives on the church fathers' beliefs regarding women*, concludes that, "Women belonged to the carnal world and were primarily characterised by lust and defined by their sexuality and were often viewed to be more libidinous than men. The church fathers therefore warned men against temptresses who continuously reproduced Eve's initial temptation of Adam. It is important to note here that women were not viewed to be temptresses out of desire, but that they were viewed as temptresses as part of their carnal nature."[12]

The Christian fundamentalist perspective of the nineteenth century had behind its sails the winds of more than two thousand years of misogynist tradition. Just three months after that day in May, 1919 which Sutton identifies as the day when American fundamentalism was born, women in the United States achieved the right to vote. Every advance made by women since that moment has sent shock waves through the male dominated fundamentalist establishment.

In March, 2021, The *New York Times* reported on the exodus of Southern Baptist Bible teacher and speaker, Beth Moore, from the Southern Baptist Church. Since the election of Donald Trump in 2016, Moore has confronted the racism and sexism of the denomination, as well as what she perceives as the mishandling of sexual abuse cases in the church. "There comes a time when you have to say, this is not who I am," said Moore. "I am still a Baptist, but I can no longer identify with Southern Baptists."[13]

In a denomination where women are not allowed to become ministers, one Southern Baptist clergyman opined:

"The fact that Beth Moore joyfully promotes herself as a woman who preaches to men is only the tip of the iceberg of her problematic positions," Tom Buck, senior pastor of First Baptist Church of Lindale, Texas, said in a post online following the news.

"I sincerely wish Mrs. Moore had repented rather than left," he wrote. "But if she refuses to repent, I am glad she is gone from the S.B.C. [Southern Baptist Convention] Sadly, leaving the S.B.C. won't fix what is wrong with Beth Moore."[14]

So what is "wrong with" Beth Moore? She is an intelligent, powerful woman who wants to speak and teach what she believes in a misogynist religious subculture.

In fundamentalist Christianity, misogyny is assumed and has become even more virulent since the advent of Trumpism. Jeff Jansen, co-founder of the Global Fire Ministries International in Murfreesboro, Tennessee, and self-proclaimed "prophet," is now disparaging pastors for being "effeminate." Jansen declared that "the church, the Ecclesia, the government of God, has been so neutered and so turned effeminate, *almost homosexual*, I'm just telling you straight up. Straight up. It's ridiculous... Where are the men? Where's the maleness?" Jansen boasts that men in his church carry guns. "The ushers at my church, they all pack," Jansen said. "If you come to my place and you think about starting something? You're dead. They'll kill you. They'll shoot you because they're going to protect everybody else." He boasted as well that he had given his armed ushers "a license to kill."[15]

As I will argue in more depth in a subsequent chapter on the psychology of fundamentalism, not only has women's equality been fervently resisted by male evangelicals, so has all gender diversity—lesbian, gay, bisexual, and transgender orientation, as well as the right of women to control their bodies through abortion. From the perspective of Christian fundamentalist doctrine, the pinnacle of holy and biblically-sanctioned sexuality has always been and continues to be heterosexual activity in marriage between a man and woman, each spouse arriving in the marriage with explicit heterosexual virginity.

THE HEAVENLY ATM

Technological advances, particularly in the 1980s, brought us the advent of televangelism and the megachurch, that is, a Protestant, evangelical church with an unusually large membership that also offers a variety of educational and social activities. Whereas the Christian evangelists such as Billy Sunday, Oral Roberts, and Billy Graham conducted their religious rallies in tents or stadiums because local churches were unable to accommodate large crowds, the megachurch is a local church, a concert and religious rally venue, and a performing arts center. In megachurches, hundreds or thousands of people attend regular Sunday services as well as concerts, special rallies with traveling evangelists who draw record-breaking crowds, and any or all of these activities can be televised and broadcast around the world. No longer confined to radio broadcasting or recordings of its activities, the outreach of Christian fundamentalism has grown exponentially since the post-World War I era.

Driven by the Biblical imperative to evangelize and superbly motivated by capitalist sensibilities, mass evangelism has morphed into a fundamentalist Christian empire. Whereas the earliest fundamentalists in America were working class believers who dropped their dollars and coins into the collection plate on Sunday or at a revival meeting, the modern believer has a variety of options for contributing to their favorite evangelical corporation. Most lucrative for pastors and most convenient for members of the megachurch or televangelism audience is the use of credit cards, or even better, committing to a monthly deduction from bank accounts.

In January, 2021, Showbiz Cheatsheet listed the top ten richest preachers in the United States. Joyce Meyer, one of the few female televangelists, has a net worth of $8 million. She's followed by Franklin Graham, son of Billy Graham, whose net worth is $10 million. Coming in at $20 million is T.D. Jakes and then Rick Warren at $25 million, then an evangelist with a fascinating last name, Creflo Dollar, at $27 million. Israeli-born Benny Hinn with his Miracle Crusades weighs in at $60 million, while the baby-faced Joel Osteen, pastor of the largest Protestant Church in America and the long-time televangelist, Pat Robertson, both carry a net worth of $100 million. However, the Croesus of them all is Kenneth Copeland with his airstrip and private jets who registers a net worth of $300 million.[16]

Proponents of the prosperity gospel preach tithing or giving ten percent of one's income each month to "the Lord's work." Kenneth Copeland explains it well, according to Burton, who writes: "Thus could Ken Copeland write in his *Laws of Prosperity*, 'Do you want a hundredfold return on your money? Give and let God multiply it back to you. No bank in the world offers this kind of return! Praise the Lord!'"[17]

The American evangelical movement was created by people from humble beginnings. However, with the elimination of the Great Depression by the economic policies of Franklin Roosevelt, which Christian fundamentalists perceived as a threatening alignment with the social gospel, they united both economically and theologically to oppose what they perceived as a socialist, anti-capitalist trend in America.

Frances Fitzgerald clarifies that "during the 1950s fundamentalists divided into two camps, corresponding to the two conflicting impulses present in fundamentalism since its inception: one to guard doctrinal purity without compromise; the other to reclaim America and to gain the world for Christ through revivals. Virtually all fundamentalists believed in both courses of action, but in the 1940s many felt they had to make choices, and the two impulses materialized in the form of two parties: one separatist, militant, and often politically extremist; the other inclusivist, bent on regaining respectability and cultural influence, preferring to be called "evangelical" as opposed to 'fundamentalist.' The two parties were, however, not completely distinct, for both came out of the crucible of the fundamentalist-modernist controversy."[18]

As stated by Sutton above, a leading organizer of the fundamentalist campaign against the social gospel in the United States was William Bell Riley, a Baptist theologian based in Minneapolis, where his Northwestern Bible and Missionary Training School (1902), Northwestern Evangelical Seminary (1935), and Northwestern College (1944) produced thousands of graduates. At a large conference in Philadelphia in 1919, Riley founded the World Christian Fundamentals Association (WCFA), which became the chief interdenominational fundamentalist organization in the 1920s. Some, like Sutton, mark this conference as the public start of Christian fundamentalism. Although the fundamentalist drive to take control of the major Protestant denominations failed at the national level during the 1920s, the network of churches and missions fostered by Riley showed that the movement was growing in strength, especially in the U.S. South. Both rural and urban in character, the flourishing movement acted as a denominational surrogate and fostered a militant evangelical Christian orthodoxy. The Independent Fundamental Churches of America became a leading association of independent U.S. fundamentalist churches upon its founding in 1930. As a result, the American

Council of Christian Churches was founded for fundamental Christian denominations as an alternative to the National Council of Churches, which consisted primarily of nonfundamentalist churches and proponents of the social gospel.

In her Yale University doctoral dissertation, Mary Hammond notes:

> Businessmen played a unique role as mediators between the evangelical subculture, to which they brought money and organizational skills, and the broader culture, to which they witnessed their faith....R.G. LeTourneau, a self-taught engineer who built a manufacturing company during the Depression, transformed his corporate platform into a pulpit. A blunt, quick-witted tornado of a man, his head permanently tilted atop a towering frame that survived two neck-breaking accidents, LeTourneau embodied a "God-fearing, hustling, successful, two-fisted Regular Guy." When evangelical businessmen stressed their status as laymen, as LeTourneau often did, it was to reject the implied mirror image of a cloistered, out-of-touch, effeminate minister. This gendering of roles, which countless collaborations and friendships belied, brought corporate divisions of labor and expertise into religious life. Just as businessmen felt unqualified to dissect Biblical passages in the original Hebrew, they doubted clerical competence in the rough-and-tumble realm of public affairs.[19]

Groups such as the Christian Business Men's Committee International (CBMCI), the Business Men's Evangelistic Clubs (BMEC), and the Gideons believed that businessmen were God's instruments to Christianize the world. As salesmen, they saw themselves as a cadre of expert manipulators. If they could convince the masses to buy their products, then they must try to bend them to God's will...The CBMCI, BMEC, and Gideons rejoiced that God was giving America the power to evangelize every soul in the world.

The Christian Business Men's Committee International, the Christian Laymen's Crusade, and the Gideons did much to institutionalize 'revivalism as politics' during the 1930s and 1940s. Evangelical businessmen's groups formed around a single, specific, and, they believed, timeless purpose, that of winning converts and helping churches to keep them. During the 1950s, former Fuller Brush salesman Billy Graham was catapulted to fame and fortune by a number of Christian businessmen and evangelists who were passionately invested, both financially and theologically, in creating a vast Christian evangelism bulwark.[20] Subsequently, from the 1930s until the 1980s, with the advent of televangelists such as Pat Robertson, Jerry Falwell, Sr., and Jim and Tammy Faye Bakker, the prosperity gospel was and continues to be the lifeblood of the fundamentalist Christian empire in the United States.

Understanding the racism, sexism, and economic greed inherent in Christian fundamentalism is essential as we journey more deeply into the psychology of the movement—how it has been shaped by American culture in the twentieth and twenty-first centuries, and how it has enabled its members and others in the culture at large to take comfort in its preferred version of social and political fascism.

3. THE PSYCHOLOGY OF CONTEMPORARY CHRISTIAN FUNDAMENTALISM

Over the years and continuing to this day the various rigid religions in the world have caused great pain and conflict among people. The very nature of dogma is to separate, because these kinds of systems claim to have the only truth. Therefore, no matter how altruistic its announcements, a rigid religion will produce judgment, because there will always be "others" who believe differently. Judgment leads to discrimination and, all too often, to persecution. Dogma can never bring us together to understand each other in our shared humanity.
—Marlene Winell, Psychologist, author of
*Leaving the Fold: A Guide for Former Fundamentalists
and Others Leaving Their Religion*[1]

I believe that my parents' call to the ministry actually drove them crazy... I think religion was actually their source of tragedy.
—Frank Schaeffer, author of
Why I Am An Atheist Who Believes in God[2]

At this point the reader may argue that Christian fundamentalism has contributed many positive and life-supporting things to humanity. One may argue that because of the efforts of fundamentalist missionaries in developing countries, schools, hospitals, and small businesses have been established. People have been educated, lives have been saved, and the status of women and children has been dramatically improved as a result of massive efforts to evangelize villages and even entire countries. Isn't the conversion of a drug addict, intent on committing a host of crimes, including murder, preferable to allowing him or her to believe whatever they want to believe and behave however they wish to behave?

That the efforts to evangelize throughout the world have saved and improved lives is irrefutable. Not every fundamentalist Christian achievement has been damaging, but I would argue that nearly every achievement exacts a price that overwhelmingly damages the human spirit through racism, colonialization, misogyny, economic exploitation, and myriad forms of abuse.

Christian fundamentalism is a dramatic departure from the teachings of Jesus in the New Testament. It was a profound reaction to the psychological trauma of dizzying changes in nineteenth and twentieth-century culture that religion could no longer contain. It is worth emphasizing that Jesus did not specialize in control, but preferred calm discernment over hysterical reaction—"Not my will but thine be done." The surrender of one's ego and the relinquishment of control is risky. What if my culture embraces all that personally threatens me? For fundamentalists in the nineteenth century, Jesus' method was weak and hazardous, as noted above in the story of R.G. LeTourneau and the Christian Businessmen's Committee. Perhaps it was safer to worship Jesus than to model him. Perhaps in the capitalist milieu of the industrial revolution, it was easier to embrace a new-birth experience as a kind of celestial insurance policy for residence in heaven after this life than to engage in the struggle that following Jesus' example of mercy, compassion, justice, and integrity in human affairs would demand.

While fundamentalists rejected the transcendentalist philosophers of the nineteenth century, they were subtly seduced into one aspect of that philosophy by reverting to the medieval paradigm of viewing this world as a vale of tears that the faithful must strive to "rise above." Being fully human and engaging with the messiness of life is not the exalted status to which the human ego believes it is entitled. *The crux of all religious trauma is the delusion that one can and should transcend the human condition.*

When an individual or a culture opts for control as opposed to compassion, discernment, and wisdom, some form of abuse is almost inevitable. Children and women will be abused. Nature, from which one feels increasingly estranged in an industrial society, will be exploited and eventually destroyed, particularly if one assumes that humans have dominion over it. Animals will be captured and tortured in the name of food supply and commercial profit. Religion will become an industry of soul-saving and fundraising at the expense of human sanity and human needs.

A SYSTEMATICALLY ABUSIVE SYSTEM

Shamelessly and with good authority, I assert that Christian fundamentalism is as inherently abusive as the fundamentalism of any other religion or militant belief system. It is inherently violent, beginning with the assertion that Jesus was tortured and murdered for your or my individual sins. The Bible itself is replete with stories of abuse and people who condoned myriad forms of it. With its belief in the subjugation of women and children, Christian fundamentalism provides fertile ground for the physical, sexual, emotional and spiritual abuse of other human beings. Moreover, in Christian fundamentalist circles, one will be hard-pressed not to encounter individuals who have suffered one or more of these forms of abuse. In fact, it is my firm belief, based on my own experiences and those of countless individuals who have survived growing up in fundamentalist households, that Christian fundamentalism is itself a band aid for the many forms of abuse that its adherents have suffered— and that many have inflicted on others despite their own abuse histories.

What is more—how can we fail to notice the abusive nature of fundamentalist theology itself, which declares that every human being is inherently sinful simply by way of being born into a body? The body is sinful because it is an instrument of one's sinful nature. Every human is destined for an eternity in hell after this life unless she or he has accepted Jesus as their personal savior and experienced the new birth. Yet, even the new birth does not eliminate the sinful nature. One must strictly follow fundamentalist Christian teaching in order to prevent sinning, even after conversion. Even though one is assured of heaven after death, one must constantly monitor one's thoughts and behavior to avoid sin. Certain activities and lifestyles must be strictly avoided because they are sinful and disapproved of by Biblical teaching. Until one arrives in heaven after death, one will never be free of sin, so one must be constantly vigilant. A person cannot trust their thoughts or feelings, but must constantly ask God to guide them. To relax into their humanity, to cut themselves some slack for being human, or to think too highly of themselves is to start down the slippery slope of sin that could result in bringing some form of adversity on them. In fact, whenever a person experiences adversity, they must always ask how they may have brought it upon themselves through sinful behavior.

How is what I have just described *not* self-abusive? How is it not judgmental, harsh, and profoundly disrespectful of one's humanity? At worst, it is cruel, and at best it is unkind.

Ultimately, such self-recrimination harms not only oneself, but all with whom one interacts. If I am constantly managing my own tendency to sin, I will invariably be managing yours. And that is precisely what Christian fundamentalism became— an elaborate sin-management program that fears and invariably loathes humanity and the human condition.

One of the hallmarks of fundamentalist Christianity is systemic abuse. Children are indoctrinated with shame and self-loathing, and they often spend their entire lives from cradle to grave attempting to escape their shame, foist it on others, or both. The born-again experience frequently provides a salve or elixir for being a long-term victim of abuse on the one hand, or a malicious perpetrator of abuse on the other.

ORIGINAL SIN, ORIGINAL SHAME

Perhaps nothing is more foundational in Christian fundamentalism than original sin. Incessantly quoted is Romans 3:23, written by the Apostle Paul: "For all have sinned and come short of the glory of God." (KJV) If we look closely, we see that Paul did not say that humans are originally sinful, but that all have sinned. In other words, all human beings have committed sin and fallen short of God's glory at some time in their lives. The passage does not argue for original sin or the notion that humans were born sinful, nor did Jesus ever teach original sin. It was not until the third century C.E. that Augustine argued for the concept.[3]

Original sin is inherent in the sin-management system, and it invariably creates and maintains a psychological and spiritual malignancy of shame within every believer. Whereas a devout fundamentalist parent may shame a child for fighting or stealing or masturbating, these acts are not the ultimate rationale for shaming the child. A child "deserves" to be shamed because he or she was born sinful. Regardless of how well-behaved, virtuous, kind, considerate, or obedient a child is, they were born sinful, and fundamentalist teaching never allows a child to forget that underlying shame, even if it is rarely verbalized, because fundamentalist teaching itself rests on the inherent sinfulness of being born into a human body.

Therefore, it is axiomatic that the body is inherently sinful, particularly the genitals, which serve no purpose other than elimination of waste and reproduction. Any other genital activity is sinful. Masturbation is sinful, same-gender attraction is sinful, and heterosexual sex before marriage is sinful. In fact, sexual pleasure for its own sake is sinful.

Most shameful is the female body that menstruates and gives birth.

In the third century, Christian theologian Tertullian wrote about women:

And do you not know that you are (each) an Eve? The sentence of God on this sex of yours lives in this age: the guilt must of necessity live too. You are the devil's gateway: you are the unsealer of that (forbidden) tree: you are the first deserter of the divine law: you are she who persuaded him whom the devil was not valiant enough to attack. You destroyed so easily God's image, man. On account of your desert—that is, death—even the Son of God had to die. And do you think about adorning yourself over and above your tunics of skins?[4]

Also in the third century, Augustine wrote:

Watch out that she does not twist and turn you for the worse. What difference does it make whether it is in a wife or in a mother, provided we nonetheless avoid Eve in any woman?[5]

Martin Luther stated in the sixteenth century:

> For woman seems to be a creature somewhat different from man, in that she has dissimilar members, a varied form and a mind weaker than man. Although Eve was a most excellent and beautiful creature, like unto Adam in reference to the image of God, that is with respect to righteousness, wisdom and salvation, yet she was a woman. For as the sun is more glorious than the moon, though the moon is a most glorious body, so woman, though she was a most beautiful work of God, yet she did not equal the glory of the male creature.[6]

The Bible is replete with references to women as seductive, inferior beings who are always ready and willing to lead men astray with treachery, sexual desire, and manipulation.

COULD FUNDAMENTALISM FUNCTION WITHOUT SHAME?

In his article, "The Church Needs Shame To Function," author and poet Dan Foster argues that without shame, the Christian church could not function. I find his theory particularly relevant to fundamentalist Christianity, as he notes several ways in which manipulation through shame is essential.

1. Shame is necessary in order to accomplish conversion. It almost always happens under duress through manipulation and the threat of spending eternity in hell unless one accepts Jesus as one's personal savior. People are not encouraged to follow Jesus because of his exemplary life and noble teachings, but are threatened with the fear of punishment.
2. Shame creates conformity. For example, shame is

used in the church to make people conform to the norms of the group. Belief, in any system, is a social exercise. Nowhere is this more evident than in the evangelical church. If you want to fit in, there are a bunch of so-called nonnegotiable "truths" that you must ascribe to. Many of them are extra-Biblical and have more to do with tradition and dogma than the actual practice of following Christ....When it comes to free-thinking, there is very little room to move in the evangelical church. People who hold to views that deviate from what is considered orthodox are most certainly shamed—both behind their backs on the gossip circuit and from the pulpit when the alarmed pastor seeks to correct your wicked heresy before it takes root and leads others astray.

3. Shame is used to generate income. As noted above, the prosperity gospel is used to incessantly preach financial contributions and especially tithing to "God's work." As Foster points out, "What is even more abhorrent than this is the suggestion that your financial giving is somehow linked to the blessing of God. The more you give, the more God will bless you, some churches will assert. In fact, your monetary gifts are capable of unlocking the blessing of God, they say. Commonly known as the 'prosperity Gospel,' this mindset insinuates that God can somehow be 'bought off' and that the blessing of God is somehow for sale."

4. Shame is used to perpetuate church attendance. In fundamentalist Christian churches, there is no such thing as going off privately to practice one's religion. From the moment of conversion, one is taught that fellowship with other believers is necessary. If you attempt to live your Christian life without it, you will invariably "go astray."

5. Shame is used to manage behavior. Listen to any fundamentalist sermon, and you are almost certain to hear, "You're doing it wrong! Get better, do better, do this more, do this less," and so on. As stated above, Christian fundamentalism is a sin-management program based in shame, and the fact is, regardless of how much one attempts to "measure up," one never will.[7]

Foster emphasizes that fundamentalist Christianity is a breeding ground for hypocrisy. "Christians are forced to pretend, repress, deny, or become a hypocrite because nothing they do will ever be good enough. It is not so much that hypocrites join churches, but that the evangelical church's very structures encourage people to act and pretend."[89] In some cases, the pressure of shame causes people to give up and leave the church, but more often, fundamentalists remain in the church for the rest of their lives and abide with the shame system.

Whereas Foster speaks of "the church," I do not cast the same kind of broad brush that he uses. I believe it is important to distinguish between fundamentalist Christian churches and nonfundamentalist, progressive churches that preach and authentically practice unconditional acceptance. The ethic of churches in the latter camp is one of inclusiveness, mercy, compassion, economic equality, and social justice.

I WILL FEAR THE LORD

Just as Christian fundamentalism cannot function without shame, in my opinion, it absolutely cannot function without fear. While it can be argued that fear permeates the Christian religion historically from the departure of Jesus from the Earth until the present day, we must always remember the historical context of fundamentalism's origins in the late nineteenth century and early twentieth century. As I have noted above, post-Civil War Christianity in America consisted of a highly traumatized population. Except for anti-slavery and abolitionist Christians in the northern states, fear of African Americans permeated white churches. To reiterate, myriad cultural changes threatened fundamentalists, and the form of Christianity they devised in those years was a mix of fear-based theology and circumscribed behavior that served to insulate them from being overwhelmed by a dizzying modernity with which they could not cope.

But more intrinsically, the bedrock of the fundamentalist theology of John Nelson Darby, William Bell Riley, C.I. Scofield, R.G. LeTourneau, and all other fundamentalists of their time was fear itself. Theirs was a God of wrath and judgment who had devised a system of rules and punishment for failing to follow the rules. Their God would punish them in this life and throughout eternity if they did not abide by the rules and dedicate their lives to convincing others that they too must think and behave, not like Jesus, but much more like the patriarchs of the Old Testament.

To commit one's life to Christian fundamentalism is to consent to a fear-based existence and the instilling of fear in others in the name of saving their souls.

When fundamentalism's implicit shame and deep-rooted fear sear the human nervous system, willful departure from the program, which promises delivery from the torture of fear and shame but severely intensifies it instead, is daunting and disorienting. In some cases, an outside cataclysm or a wrenching internal upheaval may generate the disconnection, but my experience is that people who commit to the fundamentalist path are deeply wounded, often severely abused individuals. Their conversion to the path is often a last-ditch effort to mitigate the distress of shame and fear in their personal history. Sadly, in many instances, they simply exchange one pattern of distress for another. The fundamentalist lifestyle assuages the agony of earlier wounding, but the fear and shame remain and play out in ever-new venues and more novel forms of behavior.

INTOLERABLE UNCERTAINTY

John Pierce, author and editor of Good Faith Media, stated in his article, *Certainty is the Root of All Fundamentalist Problems*:

> The corners in which fundamentalists so often find themselves —whether pushed by science, love, common sense or the public exposure of their sins—are of their own making. They are dark corners that allow for no light, no fresh revelation—as if the Spirit of God is no longer at work...Truth can only be seen in the past tense as expressed in the fragile faith of fundamentalist absolutes that give them absolute power. It is an entrenched religion more than a living faith...So when long-term, overwhelming scientific revelations or societal shifts force them to acknowledge misinterpretation of biblical truth—such as in the case of slavery—they keep the matter in the past tense so that blame rests only with their ancestors. Most tragically, there is never a confession of even the possibility of being wrong in the present...False certainty makes confession of errant belief very, very hard—although confession is vital for spiritual well-being. And even more difficult is the capacity to admit one might be wrong about something currently or in the future. For fundamentalists to do so would be to say that God was wrong—since they have conflated their faulty doctrinal positions with divine directives—and defended their poor biblical interpretations as God's absolutes. Such certainty is certainly sin.[10]

Apologetics is a branch of Christian theology that

defends Christianity against objections. Every fundamentalist Bible college or theological seminary offers, and sometimes requires, apologetics courses. Almost from the moment of "accepting Jesus as one's personal savior," converts are encouraged to "defend the faith." I believe that the inconsistencies and contradictions in the fundamentalist world view, not to mention encouragement from clergy and Bible teachers, require believers to constantly upgrade their apologetics aptitude. However, I would also argue that the believer is not only defending the faith by warding off an external enemy, but building ever-stronger intellectual bulwarks to conquer their own doubts.

Fundamentalist preaching and teaching are brimming with military metaphors and imagery. Never far from a devout fundamentalist consciousness is Ephesians 6:12 (KJV), "For we wrestle not against flesh and blood, but against principalities, against powers, against the rulers of the darkness of this world, against spiritual wickedness in high places." From this perspective, the world is inherently adversarial because it desires to eliminate the Christian gospel and minimize the influence of fundamentalist Christians. Therefore, the well-trained "Christian soldier" must be a master of apologetics who can defend the faith.

Again, from Ephesians 6:

Put on the whole armour of God, that ye may be able to stand against the wiles of the devil. For we wrestle not against flesh and blood, but against principalities, against powers, against the rulers of the darkness of this world, against spiritual wickedness in high places. Wherefore take unto you the whole armour of God, that ye may be able to withstand in the evil day, and having done all, to stand. Stand therefore, having your loins girt about with truth, and having on the breastplate of righteousness; and your feet shod with the preparation of the gospel of peace; above all, taking the shield of faith, wherewith ye shall be able to quench all the fiery darts of the wicked. And take the helmet of salvation, and the sword of the Spirit, which is the word of God: praying always with all prayer and supplication in the Spirit, and watching thereunto with all perseverance and supplication for all saints (6:11-18).

A skilled fundamentalist "soldier" cannot afford to be uncertain. He or she must be able to cite chapter and verse in the Bible which defends the faith or causes the unbeliever to tremble. Ambiguity cannot be tolerated. All of the answers are in the 66 books of the Bible, and if the Christian soldier cannot find them there, then they must pray for guidance and adhere to the faith in the meantime.

Since there must be no ambiguity, there must be no uncertainty—no gray areas. The hue of the terrain is black and white only. Armed with the scriptures which hold all of the answers, an arrogant mental posture is inevitable. *I have the truth; you don't. I am en route to heaven; you are en route to hell. I have a direct trunk line to God; you are separated from God—baffled and manipulated by the devil.* If you have ever been the prey of a fundamentalist preacher or pamphlet or video ad or door to door evangelist or a proselytizing television commercial, you will recognize this particular variety of arrogance by the way it insults and suffocates your sensibilities—unless, of course, your self-esteem is so debased and your mood so self-effacing that it will sound like music to your ears. In fact, Christian evangelism often appeals to individuals whose self-esteem is severely damaged or who carry so much shame that they find the so-called forgiveness of the born-again experience irresistible.

If you are put off by the fervor in these evangelistic appeals, it is important to remind yourself of the fragility inherent in them. While you may be offended by the audacious assumption that you are a "lost soul" desperately seeking salvation, know that the intrusiveness of the appeal disguises the vulnerability in those who are appealing. For all the fervent bombast, the ones whose mission in life it is to convert *you* desperately need to do so in order to convert themselves over and over and over again. In other words, their spiritual assault on your soul has nothing to do with you and everything to do with their own wavering acceptance of what they are proclaiming.

This is yet another form of abuse in which the mental and sometimes personal space of the "lost soul" is intruded upon. In this worldview, the "lost soul" is never viewed as an equal—a fellow member of the human race who has a right to believe what they choose to believe. Rather, the "lost soul" is an infidel in violation of God's will because they do not have a personal relationship with Jesus. Whereas within the framework of radical Islam, the infidel must be eliminated, within the framework of Christian fundamentalism, he or she must be converted in order to avoid being eliminated by God.

As I will address below, this is why it is futile to attempt to engage in meaningful dialog with Christian fundamentalists. No dialog can be productive as long as one person assumes the position of savior while viewing the other as the infidel.

BE NOT OF THIS WORLD

As noted above, the born-again experience of accepting Jesus as one's personal savior not only serves as an insurance policy for spending eternity in heaven after leaving this Earth, it also instills a posture of separation from the rest of humanity and the human condition. Although the born-again believer may be required to experience the vicissitudes of the human condition, unlike the unbeliever, they will be able to experience them as spiritual trials or tests that will make the believer stronger in their faith. Nevertheless, in this world view, the believer has a "special" relationship with God and will for the rest of their life, and they must act accordingly, always obeying the command to be mindful of the difference between themselves and the world.

Perhaps the clearest and most direct of these commands is the one from Paul in Romans 12: "Do not be conformed to this world, but be transformed by the renewal of your mind, that by testing you may discern what is the will of God, what is good and acceptable and perfect." Or another command from Paul written to the Philippians: "But our citizenship is in heaven, and from it we await a Savior, the Lord Jesus Christ, who will transform our lowly body to be like his glorious body, by the power that enables him even to subject all things to himself." (Philippians 3:20-21) And from the Apostle John, "Do not be surprised, brothers, that the world hates you."(I John, 3:13)

Whereas equality, kinship, similarity, and reciprocity were central to Jesus' teachings, as the disciples of Jesus began to spread his teachings far and wide in places where the Christian story posed a threat to various religious and political systems, Christian teachers such as the apostles were persecuted and killed for their allegiance to Jesus. All of the apostles were martyred, and countless Christian converts were fed to the lions in Rome.

Jesus had instructed his followers to forgive hostility and persecution and to continue holding everyone in their hearts as children of God, no matter how severely they were mistreated for their allegiance to Jesus. In this context, Jesus said, "Suppose ye that I am come to give peace on earth? I tell you, Nay; but rather division."(Luke 12:51) He did not prefer division, but he knew division would be the inevitable result of his teachings which were so opposed to the brutality, greed, hatred, and hypocrisy of his day. Taking a stand for equality and social justice always brings division and persecution, as Martin Luther King, Jr. and his allies quickly discovered.

Therefore, the command "be not of this world" in the context of hostility toward and persecution of the early Chris-

tians makes sense. What does not make sense and is incompat-
ible with Jesus' teachings is the manner in which fundamentalist
Christianity dichotomized humanity on the basis of the born-
again experience. Those who have accepted Jesus as personal
savior are the "us," and those who have not been born again are
the "them" or "the world."

Western civilization is based on the story of separation from
nature, from the Earth community, from the body, and the soul.
After all, did not God say, "Let us make man in our image, after
our likeness: and let them have dominion over the fish of the
sea, and over the fowl of the air, and over the cattle, and over all
the earth, and over every creeping thing that creepeth upon the
earth"? (Genesis 1:26-28 KJV)

Today, in what may be the beginning of the end of the
human species on Earth, we are starting to experience the
horrific consequences of "dominion" over nature. As Helen
Ellerbe writes in *The Dark Side of Christian History*, "In Christian
eyes, the physical world became the realm of the devil....Time,
once thought to be cyclical, like seasons, was now perceived to
be linear."[11] The pagan traditions of nature-based religions were
incorporated into very early Christianity, then later rejected as
"false teachings." One essential element of these traditions was
reverence for the body as an extension of nature. Dancing, an
integral part of pagan religions and their celebrations, was
particularly offensive to orthodox Christians. Sir John of Salisbury, a twelfth-century Bishop of Chartres, wrote,

> Who except one bereft of sense would approve sensual pleasure
> itself, which is illicit, wallows in filthiness, is something that
> men censure, and that God without doubt condemns? For since
> these two forms of physical delight, gluttony and carnal love,
> are characteristic of beasts, the one seems to possess the filth of
> swine and the other the stench of goats.[12]

Following the death of Jesus, Christianity became an enormous factor in humanity's alienation from the natural world and the emotions. Two thousand years later, Christian fundamentalism drew an additional red line between "us and them" in its obsession with the born-again experience. In other words, the theme of our common humanity was eclipsed by the concept of "the saved" and "the unsaved."

THE BIRTH OF THE RELIGIOUS RIGHT

As we have seen, the rise of fundamentalism was in part a response to cultural changes that threatened both Christians and non-Christians. While the movement grew in the late nineteenth and early twentieth centuries, it was never fully embraced by the established Christian denominations or by either of the major political parties. Yes, Billy Graham and his Minneapolis-based evangelistic association grew in popularity and claimed millions of converts in the 1940s, '50's, and '60's, but it was always somewhat of a fringe element. Certainly, no American president had facilitated the burgeoning of Christian fundamentalism—until Ronald Reagan took office in 1981.

Although Reagan was not a fundamentalist, he was certainly evangelical-friendly, and his political views resonated with those on the Republican right. "The evangelical presidency: Reagan's dangerous love affair with the Christian right," a 2014 *Salon Magazine* article by Steven Miller, details how Reagan's landslide victory in 1980 made the Moral Majority a force to be reckoned with in American politics.[13] While Reagan did not state forthrightly that he was a born-again Christian, the Religious Right made a strategic decision to align themselves with him because in so many instances, his policies and theirs were nearly identical: "trickle-down" economics, stereotypes of the poor and minorities as "welfare Cadillac recipients," macho militarism, opposition to abortion, and turning a blind eye to the HIV/AIDS epidemic. Jerry Falwell and the Moral Majority movement spearheaded media campaigns to get Reagan elected, and Reagan's victory greased the wheels of a televangelism industry that America had never before experienced.

HOLY HEROIN AND THE CHARISMATIC CRUTCH

The birth of the Religious Right was a birth not only of uber-conservative Republicanism, but a groundswell of the Pente-costal and Charismatic fundamentalism that represented an uber-conservative Christianity. Pentecostalism is a type of Christian fundamentalism that emphasizes direct personal experience of God through baptism with the Holy Spirit. The term *Pentecostal* is derived from Pentecost, an event that commemorates the descent of the Holy Spirit upon the followers of Jesus Christ, and the speaking in "foreign" tongues as described in the second chapter of the Acts of the Apostles in the New Testament.[14]

"Baptism with the Holy Spirit" is not a traditional baptism where water is used. "Baptism" is used symbolically to mean that one has become "filled with" or "overcome with" the Holy Spirit, the third person of the Christian trinity. "Speaking in foreign tongues" occurs with the baptism and is an indication that it has taken place. It should be emphasized that these "tongues" are not an actual language. I have been present in Pentecostal church services, and I can verify that speaking in tongues is actually garbled gibberish that people ecstatically utter when they are "under the influence" of the Holy Spirit. The entire process, being baptized with the Holy Spirit and speaking in tongues, is a very emotional experience. A person who wants to receive the baptism usually does so when they are in a state of euphoria, longing to feel closer to God or be over-taken by the presence of God. The experience usually takes place in a church service with emotional music playing, people singing songs, praying loudly, and praising God. The baptism usually occurs after a minister has preached a sermon and people are invited to come to the front of the church and be born again, or if they are already born again, receive the baptism of the Holy Spirit.

Essentially, there are two kinds of fundamentalist churches: One kind does not practice the baptism of the Holy Spirit, such as a Southern Baptist church, and the other kind does, such as a Pentecostal church which may be part of the Assembly of God, Apostolic Church of God, Full Gospel, or Vineyard denominations.

Indeed, an entire series of books could be written on the Pentecostal phenomenon, but my intention is to focus at this juncture on its role in the psychology of fundamentalism. The Pentecostal movement within fundamentalist Christianity has grown exponentially in the United States since the 1980s. A 2014 *Christianity Today* article asks, "Why Do These Pentecostals Keep Growing?"[15] The article addresses the sociological, rather than the theological, reasons. First, the "spirit-filled" or baptism of the Holy Spirit experience is an enormous factor. Secondly, those who have had the experience want to share it with others who have had the experience. Thirdly, people who join Pentecostal churches prefer the passion, the ecstasy, the fire-in-the-belly devotion of their denomination to what they see as the "blandness" of non-Pentecostal evangelical churches. And finally, as all fundamentalists do, they want to save souls, and they believe that non-believers are more easily attracted to the emotion of a charismatic church (from the word "charisma") than a well-behaved, noncharismatic evangelical church.

It is not difficult to see that the baptism of the Holy Spirit experience reinforces the fundamentalist perception of "us" and "them" explained above. It is one thing to be a born-again Christian, which makes one very special; it is even more extraordinary to be a born-again Christian who has been baptized with the Holy Spirit. For the charismatic Christian, one is not only "not of this world," but one is also a bit above and beyond the non-charismatic Christian.

The shame-based fear of being judged as less devout, being more worldly, not being as pure as one should be, not investing as much time and energy in the church, not attending church often enough, and not modeling an impeccable white Christian paragon of godly behavior is intensified in Pentecostal churches. However, Pentecostal or not, the devout born-again Christian lives in constant fear of sinning or not living up to the moral standard that he, she, or their church believes is the ideal. Any hint of attraction to someone of the same gender or sexual behavior with anyone before marriage is anathema. Modest dress codes for women in many Pentecostal churches and discouraging contraception entirely is typical.

Dr. Marlene Winell grew up in a fundamentalist Christian home, raised by missionary parents. She now writes and teaches about Christian fundamentalism and the "Religious Trauma Syndrome"(RTS) which is the condition experienced by people who are struggling with leaving an authoritarian, dogmatic religion and coping with the damage of indoctrination. They may be going through the shattering of a personally meaningful faith and/or breaking away from a controlling community and life-style. RTS is a function of both the chronic abuses of harmful religion and the impact of severing one's connection with one's faith.

On her website she lists the symptoms of religious trauma:

- Cognitive: Confusion, poor critical thinking ability, negative beliefs about self-ability and self-worth, black and white thinking, perfectionism, difficulty with decision-making
- Emotional: Depression, anxiety, anger, grief, loneliness, difficulty with pleasure, loss of meaning

- Social: Loss of social network, family rupture, social
  awkwardness, sexual difficulty, behind schedule on
  developmental tasks
- Cultural: Unfamiliarity with secular world; "fish out
  of water" feelings, difficulty belonging, information
  gaps (e.g., evolution, modern art, music)

She also lists the causes of the RTS syndrome: Authoritarianism coupled with toxic theology which is received and reinforced at church, school, and home which results in:

- Suppression of normal child development—cognitive,
  social, emotional, moral stages are arrested
- Damage to normal thinking and feeling abilities—
  information is limited and controlled; dysfunctional
  beliefs taught; independent thinking condemned;
  feelings condemned
- External locus of control—knowledge is revealed, not
  discovered; hierarchy of authority enforced; self not a
  reliable or good source
- Physical and sexual abuse—patriarchal
  power; unhealthy sexual views; punishment used as
  discipline

Above, I have written about the abuse factors in a fundamentalist Christian milieu generally, but Winell writes more specifically:

The doctrines of original sin and eternal damnation cause the
most psychological distress by creating the ultimate double
bind. You are guilty and responsible, and face eternal
punishment. Yet you have no ability to do anything about it.
(These are teachings of fundamentalist Christianity; however,
other authoritarian religions have equally toxic doctrines.)

You must conform to a mental test of "believing" in an external, unseen source for salvation, and maintain this state of belief until death. You cannot ever stop sinning altogether, so you must continue to confess and be forgiven, hoping that you have met the criteria despite complete lack of feedback about whether you will actually make it to heaven.
Salvation is not a free gift after all.
For the sincere believer, this results in an unending cycle of shame and relief.
"...small children are biologically dependent on their adult caretakers; built into their survival mechanisms is a need to trust authority just to stay alive. Religious teachings take hold easily in their underdeveloped brains while the adults conveniently keep control. This continues generation after generation, as the religious meme complex reproduces itself, and masses of believers learn to value self-loathing and fear apocalypse."[16]

Winell isn't anti-religion so much as anti-dogma. The religious communities that cause trauma, she says, are those that prevent people from thinking for themselves and demand obedience—as opposed to those that respect differences and allow members to feel empowered as individuals. Mind control and emotional abuse may be most closely associated with cults, but "fear-based apocalyptic thinking" is a tactic that's also employed by strict religions where conformity is a must. Devout and often well-intentioned parents in these communities feel justified in their use of power tactics to brainwash their children into belief.[17]
Fundamentalist Christianity, particularly the Pentecostal version, supplies both a soporific and a stimulant for making sense of and managing the stress of our increasingly dysfunctional and destructive world. From my perspective, having witnessed my parents, who turned from traditional fundamen-

talism to Pentecostal Christianity, the psychological demands of life in the twenty-first century nudge all of us toward a variety of "narcotics," whether literal or emotional. I believe this is one of many factors that accounts for the rapid increase in membership in Pentecostal churches.

DEMONOLOGY

In a world that appears to many of us to be unraveling on every level—politically, economically, environmentally, and spiritually, it is often reassuring to be able to pinpoint a source of the chaos. Even more helpful would be the ability to rid our world of the culprits. Whereas one hundred years ago, a fundamentalist Christian may attribute the cultural upheavals that she deemed threatening to "the unsaved" who had never accepted Jesus as their personal savior, the rise of Pentecostalism in recent decades has unleashed a new form of scapegoating, namely, identifying and casting out demons. Many traditions in many cultures over millennia have practiced demonology, but casting out demons in modern Pentecostal churches is a standard procedure. From the Pentecostal perspective, one does not need an elaborate exorcism ritual, which Catholic clergy have sometimes used, as depicted in the movie *The Exorcist*. One only needs to claim their right as a spirit-filled Christian (a born-again Christian who has been baptized with the Holy Spirit) to cast out demons, because according to Pentecostal teaching, the ability to do so was one of the gifts of the original Pentecost event.

Thus, according to twenty-first century Pentecostals, the spirit-filled Christian must be vigilant about the presence of demons in the world and in their lives. Demons can cause a Christian to commit all manner of sins, such as becoming unfaithful to the church, becoming unfaithful to a spouse, engaging in sexual activity before marriage, becoming gay, lesbian, or transgender, stealing, lying, cheating, or simply losing interest in going to church. In other words, demons are constantly lurking about, waiting to entice the spirit-filled Christian away from Bible-based, Bible-sanctioned behavior, and onto the slippery slope of sin. I cannot overstate the importance of this concept because whereas the born-again Christian may succumb to temptation at any time and must remain aware of their own tendencies to commit sin, the spirit-filled Christian, or for that matter, any Christian, can be lured into sin by a demon or demons. For this reason, one must constantly pray to be protected from the influence of demons and to be able to cast them out if one feels they are being influenced by demons.

According to Pentecostal teaching, demons can also influence local, national, and world events. For example, the Trump-supporting "My Pillow" guy, Mike Lindell, says that there was evidence of Satanism in the 2020 election. Apparently, he is working with Dr. Lyle Rapacki, "who pitched himself to law enforcement agencies as an expert on devil worship during the 'Satanic Panic' of the 1980s, and who is now apparently pivoting toward being an expert in election fraud."[18]

As the statement above from Marlene Winell emphasized: "For the sincere believer, this results in an unending cycle of shame and relief." I believe that demonology and the supposed gift of being able to cast out demons provides some relief from this unending cycle of shame—because if I sin, 'the devil made me do it,' and the responsibility is not mine only. It is always easier to blame a force outside oneself than blame oneself. Therefore, I must be vigilant toward my own impulses, but I must also recognize that evil impulses are the result of demons attempting to draw me astray.

A MUSCULAR CHRISTIANITY

I often hear people who are aghast at the social and political policies of fundamentalist Christianity ask the question, "But how can they ignore the teachings of Jesus? Jesus taught compassion, mercy, forgiveness, inclusivity, and acceptance. How do they not see this?"

To that question I hasten to answer: But the teachings of Jesus are not enough, according to their dogma. They argue that just as the Old Testament without the New Testament is only half the revelation of God's plan, the teachings of Jesus are only part of the Christian story. One must include, they insist, the teachings of Jesus' apostles and of the early church fathers.

As the cultural exigencies noted above pressed upon Christianity broadly in the late-nineteenth and early twentieth centuries, both fundamentalists and modernists felt a need to revitalize their faith. As Kristin Kobes Du Mez explains in *Jesus and John Wayne: How White Evangelicals Corrupted a Faith and Fractured a Nation*, both modernists and fundamentalists in that era came to believe that Christianity needed to be masculinized. "Liberal Protestants insisted that their own social activism exemplified a manly exercise of Christianity. Fundamentalists, meanwhile, asserted that a staunch defense of doctrine evinced masculine courage and conviction, and they derided liberal theology as an effeminate squandering of the virility of true Christianity."[19]

Bursting forth on the evangelical scene in the early-twentieth century was the American baseball star, Billy Sunday, who became the most celebrated and influential American evangelist during the first two decades of the 20th century. Converting to Christianity in 1880, Sunday became a fiery and frenetic preacher whom historians sometimes perceived as a precursor to another "Billy," that is, Billy Graham, who skyrocketed to fame in the 1950s. Both men were fierce, impassioned, charismatic speakers who attracted large audiences where extended "altar calls" brought many new converts into the fold. Not only did R.G. Le Tourneau help create the Christian Businessmen's Connection, but Christian musicians like cowboy songwriters Stuart Hamblin and Redd Harper attached themselves to Billy Graham, thereby enhancing the masculinity of the fundamentalist movement.

With all of this spiritual testosterone flowing, a singular focus on Jesus' teachings in the four gospels of the New Testament would be virtually embarrassing. The diatribes of Paul, Peter, and John, bolstered by the scholarly, masculine manifestos of church fathers Augustine, Tertullian, Jerome, and Origen would moderate, yet further masculinize, the sermons of the lackluster, itinerant Jewish carpenter.

A host of books have been written on the psychology of fundamentalisms in general and Christian fundamentalism specifically. In this chapter, I have attempted to summarize what I consider the most significant aspects. One pillar of fundamentalism is that its doctrine must be broadcast to all of humanity. The command of Jesus to "go into the world and preach the gospel," also known as "the Great Commission," requires every fundamentalist Christian to evangelize in the name of Jesus. Thus, understanding the key elements of fundamentalist theology, we must necessarily consider its proselytizing initiative, which has also become a proselytizing industry.

4. BRING THEM IN FROM THE FIELDS OF SIN

And God blessed them, and God said unto them, "Be fruitful, and multiply, and replenish the earth, and subdue it: and have dominion over the fish of the sea, and over the fowl of the air, and over every living thing that moveth upon the earth."
—Genesis 1:28 (KJV)

There are hundreds of paths up the mountain, all leading to the same place, so it doesn't matter which path you take. The only person wasting time is the one who runs around the mountain, telling everyone that his or her path is wrong.
—Hindu proverb

I let go of the notion that the Bible is a divine product. I learned that it is a human cultural product, the product of two ancient communities, biblical Israel and early Christianity. As such, it contained their understandings and affirmations, not statements coming directly or somewhat directly from God. . . . I realized that whatever "divine revelation" and the "inspiration of the Bible" meant (if they meant anything), they did not mean that the Bible was a divine product with divine authority.

—Marcus Borg

The term *evangelical* derives from the Greek word *euangelion* meaning "gospel" or "good news." Technically speaking, *evangelical* refers to a person, church, or organization that is committed to the Christian gospel message that Jesus Christ is the savior of humanity. The evangelical movement in the United States began in the 1730s and was focused on "living a life that reflected personal salvation and piety instead of tradition and ritual." The most notable evangelical leaders who embraced this piety movement were Jonathan Edwards, George Whitfield, and John Wesley. Each held massive revivals that were directly responsible for Protestants in the American Colonies experiencing a "Great Awakening" and directly influenced America's founders in their establishment of the republic. [1]

What distinguishes both evangelicals and fundamentalists from mainline Protestants is the sharing of the "good news." Eighteenth-century American evangelicalism defined the good news very broadly as a way of life rather than a belief system. Fundamentalism defined the good news very narrowly: *The good news is that Jesus came to earth to die for your sins. If you accept him as your personal savior, your sins will be forgiven, and you will live eternally in heaven after death. If you do not accept him as your personal savior, you will not enter heaven after death, but instead will be sent to hell.* Both evangelicals and fundamentalists believe in the born-again experience as the central message of the good news. They also believe that the born-again experience will have an impact on one's behavior and how one lives in the world and how one relates to other individuals. Mainline Protestantism, however, does not emphasize a born-again experience and views the good news as the way to live the teachings of Jesus in the world. Progressive Protestant churches believe that each individual is already "saved" and loved unconditionally as a child of God, not needing to be born again.

As we have seen, it is the duty of every Christian who has been born again to carry the good news to the rest of the world according to a binary, us-and-them view of humanity. Fundamentalism's arrogant and often condescending stance is one of its hallmarks, but it thoroughly justifies this perspective by its interpretation of the Bible and the notion that every born-again Christian must proselytize, share the good news, and "win souls for Jesus."

People "targeted" to become converts respond in different ways when approached by someone attempting to convert them, depending on their particular psychological needs and vulnerabilities. The arrogant attitude communicated by the proselytizing fundamentalist may not offend someone who is laden with guilt, who has low self-esteem, or who is desperately in need of attention and care. In fact, it may be like music to their ears because of their psychological wounds. The fundamentalist come-on or practice of "witnessing for Christ" is literally an assault of shame. Recall that the foundation of fundamentalist teaching is that all human beings are originally and inherently sinful. Most people whose lives are working reasonably well, who feel good about themselves, or who are even somewhat religious are likely to be put off by the proselytizing tone of the zealous fundamentalist who tells them that they are sinners in need of salvation and that if they do not repent, they will spend eternity in hell. In fact, from my perspective, the more intact one's self-esteem, the more offensive the proselytizing shame-assault will be.

Although many fundamentalist sermons, televangelist broadcasts, podcasts, articles, and door-to-door evangelism crusades may be couched in "God loves you and has a wonderful plan for your life" or "here's something that can really give you peace of mind," the pitch will always result in something like "you are a sinner bound for hell, and you need to be saved."

THE MISSIONARY EMPIRE

Evangelical, fundamentalist, and Pentecostal denominations believe that once an individual has been born again, they are duty-bound to spread the good news. Drawing on the example of all of the apostles of Jesus who spread the good news throughout the then-known world and were also martyred because of their efforts, born-again Christians are committed to thinking of themselves as modern-day apostles and therefore must evangelize both locally and globally. The terms often used for this by evangelicals and fundamentalists are "witnessing for Christ," "sharing the good news," or "saving lost souls." If a Christian is not engaged in this endeavor, evangelicals and fundamentalists believe, that person should deeply examine their commitment to Christ because they are falling short of it.

The earliest Christian missionaries, as mentioned above, were the apostles, followed by a proliferation of monasteries throughout late antiquity and the Middle Ages. Monasteries provided the education and the training of priests and nuns, and also served as missionary outposts throughout Europe. During the sixteenth century, a host of explorers such as Columbus, Magellan, Drake, Balboa, DeSoto, and others conquered countless indigenous peoples throughout the world and demanded that they convert to Christianity or be tortured or killed. This set in motion a wave of colonialism by the British, French, Dutch, and Spanish, and colonialism was always attended by missionary outposts in colonized regions. According to Wikipedia, "By the 1870s Protestant missions around the world generally acknowledged that the long-term material goal was the formation of independent, self-governing, self-supporting, self-propagating churches. The rise of nationalism in the Third World provoked challenges from critics who complained that the missionaries were teaching Western ways and ignoring the indigenous culture. For example, the Boxer Rebellion in China in 1898 involved very large scale attacks on Christian missions and their converts. Later, the First World War diverted resources and pulled most Germans out of missionary work when that country lost its empire. Additionally, the worldwide Great Depression of the 1930s was a major blow to funding mission activities."[2]

Although evangelicals and fundamentalists specifically opposed the social gospel, missionaries often provided welfare and health services as good deeds or to make friends with the locals. Thousands of schools, orphanages, and hospitals were established by evangelical missions throughout the nineteenth and twentieth centuries, and while these humanitarian efforts saved lives and improved conditions for millions of individuals, they brought forced and coerced conversion to Christianity. This "carrot and stick" strategy left a toxic residue of racism, authoritarianism, the oppression of women and children, sexual abuse, environmental devastation, and uber-capitalist exploitation.

In 1934, evangelical minister and missionary, William Cameron Townsend, founded the Summer Institute of Linguistics, whose main purpose was to study, develop and document languages, especially those that are lesser-known, in order to expand linguistic knowledge, promote literacy, translate the Christian Bible into local languages, and aid minority language development. In 1942, Townsend founded Wycliffe Bible Translators that succeeded in translating the Bible into numerous native languages, which rapidly accelerated missionary efforts throughout the developing world. While evangelism of these countries was initially the primary objective of Townsend and Wycliffe Bible Translators, something else entirely happened. Gerard Colby and Charlotte Dennett document through their in-depth research the purported relationship between Nelson Rockefeller, missionaries in South America, and the modern genocide of Amazonian Indians. (*Thy Will Be Done: The Conquest of the Amazon: Nelson Rockefeller and Evangelism in the Age of Oil.*) "The authors describe the links between the SIL's (Summer Institute of Linguistics) in-depth knowledge of indigenous people and their languages and the creation of a sophisticated communications and intelligence-gathering network serving the business interests of multinational corporations and the anti-communist policies of the US government."[3]

William Cameron Townsend readily accepted large cash donations from individuals and agencies inside and outside the federal government for whom Christianity, capitalism, and anti-communism were identical battlefields. Other gifts to SIL included surplus U.S. aircraft, illegally transferred to the missionaries by the military to help the SIL penetrate the deepest parts of the jungle. [4]

In its 1995 review of Colby's and Dennett's book, the Los Angeles Times notes:

> Another narrative within *Thy Will Be Done* concerns the Amazon itself: the tragic effects of exploitation of the rain forest's resources and native peoples by missionaries, politicians and international businessmen. This horrific narrative remains unfinished. It includes the burning of irreplaceable rain forest ecosystems at the rate of an acre a minute—half the area of California every year. Huge hydroelectric dams, such as Tucurui on the Tocantins River and Balbina on the Rio Uatama, have flooded hundreds of square miles of rain forest and left behind decomposing barrels of chemical defoliant. Gold miners have stripped the hills, and iron miners are burning down acres of trees to make charcoal to run their pig-iron smelters.

This part of the book's narrative describes the even more tragic assimilation of thousands of indigenous peoples removed from their traditionally held lands and, when they resist removal, the murder of entire tribes. In Brazil alone, according to Brazilian anthropologist Darcey Ribeiro, from 1900 to 1957 more than 80 tribes were deculturated and destroyed by economic expansion. In that time, the indigenous population of Brazil fell from 1 million to less than 200,000. A Brazilian government report in 1968, conducted by attorney general Jader Figueiredo and filling 20 volumes, testified to state-sponsored persecution of indigenous Brazilians: the "massacre of whole tribes by dynamite, machine guns and sugar laced with arsenic," the deliberate introduction of infectious diseases, the prostitution of girls and mass enslavement. Commonly, these atrocities were carried out in the name of Brazil's "economic miracle." In 1976, Elie Wiesel joined other human rights advocates and scientists in protesting the world's silence concerning such genocidal programs. Today, stories continue to surface from Latin America of "ethnocide"—we would call it "ethnic cleansing" if it were in Europe—and these stories are still met predominantly with silence by the international press.

"Perhaps this is the real historical meaning of William Cameron Townsend's reaching every tribe with the Word and Nelson Rockefeller's reaching them with 'development,'" authors Colby and Dennett conclude. "Both were destructive to tribal ways of communal sharing and respect for the land. Both stories told of the same result: It was not God being brought to tribal cultures, but an alien culture of possessive individualism grown to such a giant corporate scale, with its own rapacious, competitive needs, that it could only devour them."[5]

RELIGIOUS TERRORISM

The history of Christian evangelism has been a carrot and stick melodrama in every aspect of the proselytizing process. That is not to say that conversions have always been forced, although countless conversions have been, but rather, that underlying all evangelical conversion efforts is the axiom that humans are inherently sinful and that without the born-again experience, their inevitable destiny is eternity in a literal hell. The spoken or unspoken message of the proselytizer is: "You are destined for eternal punishment in hell as a result of your sinful condition. If you accept Jesus as your personal savior, you will be spared eternal damnation and will spend eternity in heaven. We are offering you eternal salvation. If you accept it, you will be blessed on every level. If you reject it, your life will not go well, and eternal torment awaits you after death." The overt message is: "We are here to save you and improve your life." The covert message is: "If you refuse to be saved, you will be destroyed."

Within the past 60 years, fundamentalists, particularly those adhering to Scofield's Dispensation theory, as well as those in the Pentecostal movement who add their own interpretation of Biblical prophecies of the end times, have devised elaborate timelines and prognostications regarding their belief in the second coming of Jesus (the Rapture), the ensuing Battle of Armageddon, and ultimately, the destruction of the earth by God. Their uniquely manufactured interpretations of the Book of Revelation, as well as a variety of Old Testament prophecies, are routinely used to instill fear in those who have not accepted Jesus as their personal savior, as well as in their own fellow-believers. The message that "Jesus may return at any moment" attended by "will you be ready?" is both incessant and intentionally intimidating and traumatizing.

What then is the "good news"? Where is the "good" in this ultimatum? In fact, what is communicated in attempts to convert the "lost soul" is a subtle terrorism embellished with intimidation to which any self-respecting human can only respond with curiosity about what gives the proselytizer the authority to issue the ultimatum. The evangelical argues that the Bible gives him or her the authority.

The issue then becomes an issue of authority, and authority is the crux of Christofascism.

Any attempt to convert another human being to one's own world view is the imposition of one's own authority over the other, and therefore an impingement on their soul. But more to the point, what is the controversy over authority really about? Why the search for an external authority?

Several dictionaries define *authority* as the power to enforce obedience. Within the word *authority* is the word *author*. An author writes or creates something, but creating does not mean controlling others. Rather, it means controlling or taking charge of oneself. *Authoritarian* means going beyond the power to create something and into the territory of domination and control of others.

Fundamentalist Christianity is inherently authoritarian and demands that humans adhere to an external authority—religious scripture, the state, parents, teachers, political leaders, laws and law enforcement. It negates the inner authority of the human heart and the human mind because those cannot be controlled by a force outside oneself.

Authority is a necessary requirement in a liberal democracy, and indeed, any society living under the rule of law. Theoretically, laws are made by representatives of the citizenry and enforced by a justice and court system. The original intention, however, is not control, but the stability of the society and the safety of the citizenry. In the process, one is not asked to distrust one's inner authority, but to honor it alongside the rule of law, because in the end, *democracy reveres the sanctity of one's inner authority.* Authoritarian religions do not.

Issued after the violent insurrection at the Capitol in Washington, D.C. on January 6, 2021 was a new designation from the Federal Bureau of Investigation: Domestic Violent Extremism, or as we have heard on other occasions, Domestic Terrorism. Curiously, it appears that the more thoroughly we explore fundamentalist Christianity and the evangelical perspective, the more obvious are the links to American domestic terrorism.

The fundamentalist strategy has always been coercive and inherently patronizing. In fact, it is not a stretch to define it as an evangelical *jihad*. The Islamic word *jihad* literally means striving or struggling and doing so with a noble aim. Originally, the *jihad* was an internal commitment to combat one's own evil inclinations. In Sufism, which is the mystical form of Islam, this moral *jihad* was known as the "greater *jihad*" because the Sufis believed that the struggle with one's own character defects was more challenging than waging an external battle. Conversely, the nonmystical approach of some early Islamists was militant proselytization, and in the twenty-first century, we are familiar with *jihad* because of its use by Islamic terrorists to proselytize and to destroy the Judeo-Christian tradition. When we fully grasp the fundamentalist Christian *jihad*, we cannot escape its authoritarian, coercive, shaming, and emotionally and spiritually terrorist tactics. What is more, almost from its inception, fundamentalist Christianity has been a sociopolitical movement as much as it has been a religious one. And how not, since it originated in protest of nineteenth- and twentieth-century cultural trends that resulted in political actions which posed enormous spiritual and emotional threats to its belief system?

As we have seen, fundamentalists were energized, organized, and emboldened by the election of Ronald Reagan in 1980, and within a few years had formed a Religious Right movement led by Jerry Falwell Sr., Pat Robertson, Tim La Haye, Francis Schaeffer, Randall Terry, Ralph Reed, and others. The movement was further invigorated by the election of George W. Bush and the Iraq and Afghanistan wars against two Muslim countries.

In 2006, Kevin Phillips published *American Theocracy*, in which he stated:

> Christianity in the United States, especially Protestantism, has always had an evangelical—which is to say, missionary—and frequently a radical or combative streak. Some message has always had to be preached, punched, or proselytized. Once in a while that excitability has been economic—most notably in the case of the Social Gospel of the 1890s, which searched through Scripture to document the Jesus who emphasized caring for the poor and hungry. In the twentieth century, though, religious zeal in the United States usually focused on something quite different: individual pursuit of salvation through spiritual rebirth, often in circumstances of sect-driven millenarian countdowns to the so-called end times and an awaited return of Christ. These beliefs have often been accompanied by great revivals; emotionalism; eccentricities of quaking, shaking, and speaking in tongues; characterization of the Bible as inerrant; and wild-eyed invocation of dubious prophecies in the Book of Revelation. No other contemporary Western nation shares this religious intensity and its concomitant proclamation that Americans are God's chosen people and nation. George W. Bush has averred this belief on many occasions.
>
> In its recent practice, the radical side of U.S. religion has embraced cultural anti-modernism, war hawkishness, Armageddon prophecy, and in the case of conservative fundamentalists, a demand for governments by literal biblical interpretation. In the 1800s, religious historians generally minimized the sectarian thrust of religious excess, but recent years have brought more candor. The evangelical, fundamentalist, sectarian, and radical threads of American religion are being proclaimed openly and analyzed widely, even

though bluntness is frequently muted by a pseudo-tolerance, the polite reluctance to criticize another's religion. However, given the wider thrust of religion's claims on public life, this hesitance falls somewhere between unfortunate and dangerous.[6]

American Theocracy reverberated with Phillips' concerns that our formerly sectarian democracy was being subsumed by the radicalism of the Religious Right. In that same year, Chris Hedges wrote his book *American Fascists: The Christian Right and The War on America* in which he argues that "fundamentalist" or "evangelical" is no longer the correct term for members of the Religious Right who seek to institute a nation governed by Christians based on their understanding of biblical law. They are *dominionists* or *Christian reconstructionists* who "fused the language and iconography of the Christian religion with the worst forms of American nationalism and then created this sort of radical mutation, which has built alliances with powerful right-wing interests, including corporate interests, and made tremendous inroads over the last two decades into the corridors of power."[7]

Twenty-first-century fundamentalist Christians are unambiguous about who they believe should be governing America and the world: Those who have been born again, and for Pentecostal Christians, those who have been born again and have been baptized with the Holy Spirit. The counter-cultural revolution of the 1960s, the loss of the Vietnam War by the United States, the terror attacks of September 11, 2001, and the two-term election of a black President have unequivocally caused the cultural changes of the late-nineteenth and early-twentieth centuries, so formidable for fundamentalists in those days, to pale by comparison. Not only must they convert the world as quickly as possible, but they must utilize government and every institution available to that end. Moreover, they must accomplish their mission by any means necessary. What then could be more tantalizing than a white racist billionaire who claimed to be a Christian, who promised the elimination of all that has thwarted the efforts of fundamentalist Christianity, most significantly, government itself, in the advancement of racial purity, unrestrained capitalism, the elimination of abortion, marriage equality, and all manner of political correctness?

5. EVANGELICAL POLITICS

Millions of largely white Americans, hermetically sealed within the ideology of the Christian Right, yearn to destroy the Satanic forces they blame for the debacle of their lives, the broken homes, domestic and sexual abuse, struggling single parent households, lack of opportunities, crippling debt, poverty, evictions, bankruptcies, loss of sustainable incomes and the decay of their communities. Satanic forces, they believe, control the financial systems, the media, public education and the three branches of government. They believed this long before Donald Trump, who astutely tapped into this deep malaise and magic thinking, mounted his 2016 campaign for president.
—Chris Hedges[1]

Scandal does not destroy American fundamentalism. Rather, like a natural fire that purges the forest of overgrowth, it makes the movement stronger. And fiercer.
—Jeff Sharlet, *The Family: The Secret Fundamentalism at the Heart of American Power*

With the election of Ronald Reagan to the Presidency, American evangelicals began to glimpse the possibility that the wildly secularized United States would become not only more religious, but specifically, that the Reagan Presidency would facilitate seizure of the brass ring they had been craving since the onset of the evangelical movement, namely mass conversions nationally and worldwide to evangelical Christianity. Hence, the proliferation of the televangelism industry in the 1980s.

The good times were rolling in the "Me Decade" until the Jungian shadow erupted in the sexual escapades of Jim Bakker and Jimmy Swaggart. But neither scandal ultimately thwarted the mission of the Religious Right.

David Trowbridge in his *United States History, Volume 2*, asserts that:

> The challenge for the New Right was that modern politics required the mobilization of both wealth and the masses, two groups that had traditionally opposed one another. The strength of the conservative movement was its ability to weld pro-business economic policies with support for conservative social issues in a way that attracted a core group of devoted supporters *and* the backing of wealthy donors.
>
> The United States experienced a period of religious revivalism during the late 1970s and early 1980s. Similar to the Great Awakening of the early eighteenth-century, charismatic religious leaders became national celebrities and attracted legions of loyal followers. The most outspoken of these leaders were a new breed of clergy known as "televangelists" who attracted millions of loyal viewers through religious television programs. Televangelists like Billy Graham, Pat Robertson, and Jim and Tammy Faye Bakker saw their virtual congregations grow as they progressed from old-fashioned revival meetings

to radio programs and eventually popular television programs like the *700 Club*—each broadcast on several Christian cable networks.[2]

Yet all around the Religious Right, an HIV epidemic was boiling, particularly in the LGBTQ community, and Bill Clinton, pariah of the repressed righteous, was conjuring his political magic from the red state of Arkansas. At the end of Reagan's second term, his Vice-President, George Bush, Sr. was elected, running against Michael Dukakis and alongside Bob Dole, Jack Kemp, and of course, Pat Robertson. Bush, an Episcopalian, was less than dazzling for the Religious Right, but at least he was a Republican. Nevertheless, says Neil Young of the *Washington Post*, "...it was Bush, the moderate establishment Republican whose family helped found Planned Parenthood, who secured the Religious Right's permanent place in American politics. While historians largely credit Reagan's presidency with helping religious conservatives move from the shadows of American public life into its spotlight, it was the Bush presidency, particularly its disappointments and defeats, that entrenched the Religious Right as the center of the Republican Party and guaranteed its ongoing influence. In the words of Neil Young, "Religious conservatives used the Bush presidency to launch their takeover of the GOP."[3]

THE FAMILY

One of Christian fundamentalism's most calculated strategies for acquiring political power was The Family. Investigative journalist Jeff Sharlet has given us a priceless study of The Family, "a Jesus-centered, fundamentalist network whose ambitions exceed 'Al Qaeda's dream of a Sunni empire.'"[4] In his book *The Family: The Secret Fundamentalism at the Heart of American Power*, Sharlet gives us a penetrating look at Christian fundamentalism's most elite organization, which describes itself as an "invisible global network dedicated to a religion of power for the powerful." Waging spiritual warfare in the halls of Congress and around the globe, they consider themselves the "new chosen"—Congressmen, generals, and foreign dictators who meet in confidential cells to pray and plan for a "leadership led by God," to be won not by force but through quiet diplomacy.[5] Subsequently, Sharlet, a professor of English and Creative Writing at Dartmouth College, became the executive producer for a five-part Netflix documentary on The Family in 2019, which everyone who seeks to explore the "fundamentalist *jihad*" must watch.

For those who question the notion of Christo-Fascism and would argue that my use of the term is an exaggeration of Christian fundamentalist political intentions, Jeff Sharlet stated in an interview with NBC News in 2008, that he spent a month in 2002 living as an intern in a Fellowship house (maintained by The Family) near Washington, DC, during which time he wrote a magazine article describing his experiences. Sharlet stated that while living in the Fellowship house, "we were being taught the leadership lessons of Hitler, Lenin and Mao" and that Hitler's genocide "wasn't an issue for them, it was the *strength* that he emulated." Family leader Doug Coe stated that "Hitler, Goebbels and Himmler were just three men. Think of the immense power these three men had. But they bound themselves together in an agreement. Two years before they moved into Poland, these three men had systematically drawn out a plan to annihilate the entire Polish population and destroy by numbers every single house—every single building in Warsaw and then to start on the rest of Poland."[6]

Writing about The Family and the Netflix portrayal of it, Jack Seale of *The Guardian* writes:

The Fellowship has two signature moves. Its main gig is the National Prayer Breakfast (NPB), an annual invitation-only festival of speeches and meetings that has been addressed by every president since Dwight D. Eisenhower...Even less is known about the luxurious residential properties in which politicians of the present or future are invited to live communally, helping each other to find Jesus. The Family's star witness is Jeff Sharlet, the author of two books about his brief period as a resident of the pillared mansion in Virginia where the Fellowship hosts impressionable and (with the honourable exception of Sharlet) discreet young men...The Family's focus on the Fellowship hides what is really a portrait of the whole "Christian" right wing in the US—as well as the type of (white) man who has thoroughly infected western postwar politics. A stale whiff of viciously inadequate masculinity hangs over the whole show, from the young Fellows' awkwardly enforced celibacy to the episode that sets out how Fellowship missionaries have been sent to less developed countries that might be vulnerable to campaigns against gay rights. As an LGBT activist in Romania puts it: "They have a purpose in their life now. To hate you."[7]

New York Magazine's culture and entertainment website, *Vulture*, opines in its piece: "What *The Family* Reveals about white Evangelicals and Donald Trump... is that The Family 'has no problem with bad men.'" Founded by Abraham Vereide as an outreach to elites, and led by Doug Coe for decades until his death in 2017, the Family reveres power and thrives in secrecy. Before Vereide launched the National Prayer Breakfast, he sought out Nazi war criminals on orders from the U.S. State Department—and though he didn't hold Nazi beliefs, Sharlet reports that Vereide openly admired their anti-democratic discipline. In the decades since, The Family's associates have formed working relationships with some of the world's bloodiest dictators. At least one associate—former Michigan representative Mark Siljander—did time in prison in connection with these overseas activities. And Trump is just the strong man they've waited to serve. As Sharlet recalls in the Netflix series, Coe had no time for sheep and wished instead to reach the wolf. Bring in the "Wolf King," as Coe called this strong man, and you have a figure who could finally create a God-led government.

The idea that God ordains a person's place in the world is not unique to Vereide or his successor, and it has pernicious side effects. If God picks our leaders, the thinking goes, we should obey them—no matter how violent their personal lives or how vicious their political views. If you worship power, the pursuit of it becomes a sacrament. The Trump presidency is not blasphemy, then, but God's will.[8]

NO FACTS, NO PROBLEM

During the Trump era, I was incessantly asked by non-evangelicals, "How can right-wing evangelicals support Donald Trump with his vulgar, tasteless, grab-'em-by-the-pussy, boorish behavior? How can they condone his racist attitudes and contempt for the poor—so unlike the teachings of Jesus?"

From the outset of Trump's Presidency, the Christian right has used one Bible story in particular to champion Trump, in spite of his irreligious and flagrantly non-Christlike comportment.

Tara Isabella Burton, writing for *Vox*, notes that:

Many evangelical speakers and media outlets compare Trump to Cyrus, a historical Persian king who, in the sixth century BCE, conquered Babylon and ended the Babylonian captivity, a period during which Israelites had been forcibly resettled in exile. This allowed Jews to return to the area now known as Israel and build a temple in Jerusalem. Cyrus is referenced most prominently in the Old Testament book of Isaiah, in which he appears as a figure of deliverance.

While Cyrus is not Jewish and does not worship the God of Israel, he is nevertheless portrayed in Isaiah as an instrument of God—an unwitting conduit through which God effects his divine plan for history. Cyrus is, therefore, the archetype of the unlikely "vessel": someone God has chosen for an important historical purpose, despite not looking like—or having the religious character of—an obvious man of God.

For believers who subscribe to this account, Cyrus is a perfect historical antecedent to explain Trump's presidency: a nonbeliever who nevertheless served as a vessel for divine interest.[9]

Does the end justify the means? Is the Christian right willing to deploy whatever strategies lead to the conversion of more souls, the deepening of its pockets, and the triumph of its *jihad*? Just as it manipulates Biblical interpretation—declaring that passages are sometimes literal, sometimes metaphorical, sometimes mysterious, sometimes crystal clear—Christian fundamentalism is loosely attached to fact, truth, authenticity, and what is demonstrably so.

Are we then surprised that, enabled by white evangelicals, the Trump Presidency was an orgy of lies, misrepresentation, distortion, and the denial of incontrovertible reality?

While Christian fundamentalism has succeeded in undermining science in the popular worldview in terms of the reality of climate change, the validity of Covid-19 and vaccine safety, and the age of the earth and of the human species, a sufficient number of individuals have not been convinced and are, in fact, reacting to right-wing Christian politics. David Campbell, professor and chair of the University of Notre Dame's political science department and co-author of *Secular Surge: A New Fault Line in American Politics*, said that a reason for the decline among those groups is political—an "allergic reaction to the Religious Right. I see no sign that the Religious Right, and Christian nationalism, is fading. Which in turn suggests that the allergic reaction will continue to be seen—and thus more and more Americans will turn away from religion." American Atheist official Allison Gill noted that right-wing Christians "are experiencing their loss of prominence in American culture as an unacceptable attack on their beliefs—and this is driving much of the efforts we are seeing to cling onto power, undermine democracy, and fight for 'religious freedom' protections that apply only to them."[10]

New York Magazine journalist Eric Levitz opines that, "In Western Europe, the far-right White evangelical movement led by Christian fundamentalists like Pat Robertson, James Dobson, Tony Perkins and the late Moral Majority founder Jerry Falwell, Sr. didn't catch on the way it did in the United States—where White evangelicals have been a major voting block within the Republican Party. Even European Christians who go to church are likely to favor a separation of church and state and be nonfundamentalist in their views. And the U.S., according to Levitz, is moving more in that direction—much to the Christian right's dismay."

Levitz argues that as Americans become increasingly secular in their views, far-right evangelicals will respond in an authoritarian way—including voter suppression. At this writing, the latter has never been more obvious.

"Whatever its impact on the GOP," says Levitz, "the implications of creeping secularism are direr for social conservatives. The Republican Party can ultimately retain political power by bringing its policy commitments into slightly closer alignment with public opinion. That is not an option for the Christian right's true believers. As a result, the movement is becoming forthrightly anti-democratic. On the one hand, the moral minority hopes to impose its will on the nation by judicial fiat. On the other, it aims to disenfranchise the heathen majority."[11]

IN THE ABSENCE OF FACTS, VIOLENT EXTREMISM

Elizabeth Neumann is an evangelical and a former top official at the Department of Homeland Security (DHS) who resigned from Trump administration in April 2020. In her February, 2021 article in *Politico*, she warned that violent extremism and domestic terrorism are natural byproducts of Christian fundamentalism. She sees QAnon's popularity among certain segments of Christendom not as an aberration, but as the troubling-but-natural outgrowth of a particular strain of American Christianity. In this tradition, one's belief is based less on scripture than on conservative culture, some political disagreements are seen as having nigh-apocalyptic stakes, and "a strong authoritarian streak" runs through the faith. For this type of believer, love of God and love of country are sometimes seen as one and the same.[12]

Although Neumann was well aware of QAnon and other extremist groups while serving in the DHS, she was not alarmed until the outbreak of the Coronavirus pandemic. "With the pandemic," says Neumann, "you had what was perceived to be government overreach; you had social isolation, which is a known risk factor [for extremism]; you had some people with a lot more time on their hands because they were not commuting, not taking kids to ballgames and not going to happy hour after work; you had economic stress—another known risk factor—as people lost jobs or moved to part-time status; you had people who lost loved ones. There was this great sense that people had lost control; our lives as we knew them had been upended."

To her credit, Neumann is able to think critically about her faith and has not succumbed to the cult mentality of extreme Christian fundamentalism. In fact, she declares:

The authoritarian, fundamentalist nature of certain evangelical strands is a prominent theme in the places where you see the most ardent Trump supporters or the QAnon believers, because they've been told: "You don't need to study [scripture]. We're giving you the answer." Then, when Rev. Robert Jeffress [a prominent conservative Baptist pastor in Dallas] says you've got to support Donald Trump, and makes some argument that sounds "churchy," people go, "Well, I don't like Trump's language, but OK, that's the right thing." It creates people who are not critical thinkers. They're not necessarily reading scripture for themselves. Or if they are, they're reading it through the lens of one pastor, and they're not necessarily open to hearing outside perspectives on what the text might say. It creates groupthink.

Another factor is Christian nationalism. That's a huge theme throughout evangelical Christendom. It's subtle: Like, you had the Christian flag and the American flag at the front of the church, and if you went to a Christian school, you pledged allegiance to the Christian flag and the American flag. There was this merger that was always there when I was growing up. And it was really there for the generation ahead of me, in the '50s and '60s. Some people interpreted it as: Love of country and love of our faith are the same thing.[13]

THE CHRISTO-FASCIST ENDGAME

As noted above, Chris Hedges emphasizes that Christian fundamentalists are dominionists. That is, they seek to institute a nation governed by Christians based on their understanding of biblical law. In other words, they are determined to have a nation governed by their perception of God and their interpretation of the Bible, no matter what. In a 2007 appearance on *Democracy Now*, Chris Hedges stated:

...when you follow the logical conclusion of the ideology they preach, there really are only two options for people who do not submit to their authority. And it's about submission, because these people claim to speak for God and not only understand the will of God, but [to] be able to carry it out. Either you convert, or you're exterminated. That's what the obsession with the end times, with the Rapture, which, by the way, is not in the Bible, is about. It is...a fear-based movement, and it's about saying, ultimately, if you do not give up control to us, you will be physically eradicated by a vengeful God. And that lust for violence...that final aesthetic being violence is very common to totalitarian movements, the belief that massive catastrophic violence can be used as a cleansing agent to purge the world. And that's...something that this movement bears in common with other despotic and frightening radical movements that we've seen... throughout the past century.[14]

Hedges also notes the relationship between Christian fundamentalism and the Zionist movement in Israel and beyond:

...the relationship between this radical movement and the radical right in Israel is one that really brings together Messianic Jews and Messianic Christians who believe that they have been given a divine or a moral right to control one-fifth of the world's population who are Muslim. It's a really repugnant ideology. The radical Christian right in this country is deeply anti-Semitic.... [W]hen the end times come, except for the 144,000 Jews who flee to Petra and are converted...Jews will be destroyed, along with all other nonbelievers, including people like myself who are nominal Christians in their eyes. You know, there is no respect for Judaism in and of itself. It's an abstraction.... Jews have to control Israel, because that is one more step towards Armageddon. And I find that alliance strange and very shortsighted on the part of many right-wing Israelis and right-wing Jews in the United States.[15]

Fundamentalist Christians have a very schizophrenic relationship with Jews. On the one hand, they proclaim that Jews are "God's chosen people" while at the same time asserting that unless a Jew becomes a born-again Christian, they will spend eternity in hell. One fundamentalist church in San Antonio, Texas, pastored by John Hagee, preaches the "God's chosen people" theme so passionately that parishioners sometimes conduct celebrations of Jewish holidays by wearing Jewish prayer shawls and yarmulkes while dancing to traditional religious songs, even inviting Jewish congregations to join them in the festivities. Hagee famously preached a sermon on "The Nine Mysteries of the Jewish Prayer Shawl,"[16] and before the pandemic, conducted regular tours to Israel for members of his congregation. Nevertheless, Hagee asserts that if Jews do not accept Jesus as their personal savior, they will burn in hell.

By way of televangelism, foreign missionary efforts, local church outreach, or direct involvement in local, state, and national politics, Christian fundamentalism has one endgame: Domination. Whether in the bloody crusades of the Middle Ages or in the sweat-drenched Sunday rants of a megachurch evangelist, people of color must be colonized; women must be subdued; non-heterosexuals must be eliminated; nature must be conquered; white males must prevail.

Chris Hedges said it best: "Either convert, or you are exterminated."

PART II

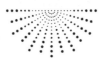

GROWING UP EVANGELICAL: HEALING THE
EVANGELICAL WOUND

6. A LITTLE KNOWLEDGE IS A DANGEROUS THING

He shall take the two goats and present them before the Lord at the doorway of the tent of meeting. Aaron shall cast lots for the two goats, one lot for the Lord and the other lot for the scapegoat. Then Aaron shall offer the goat on which the lot for the Lord fell, and make it a sin offering. But the goat on which the lot for the scapegoat fell shall be presented alive before the Lord, to make atonement upon it, to send it into the wilderness as the scapegoat. The one who released the goat as the scapegoat shall wash his clothes and bathe his body with water; then afterward he shall come into the camp.
—Leviticus 16:7-10, 26

The shadow is the block which separates us most effectively from the divine Voice.
—Carl Jung[1]

Who would ever think that so much went on in the soul of a young girl?
—Anne Frank[2]

I n the early nineteenth century, the Elkhart Prairie in
Northern Indiana was a beautiful but unforgiving place.
The land had been brutally conquered and colonized by
white settlers in the eighteenth century, and Colonel John
Jackson of Virginia moved to Elkhart County and began home-
steading along the banks of the Elkhart River. He had served in
the War of 1812 when his company followed the Indians to this
region, crossing the Elkhart River at what is now Benton, Indiana, preparing to attack the village of the Pottawatomi Indians
there. Instead, Jackson found it deserted. When he first entered
the prairie, despite his military obligations, he thought it to be
the most beautiful country he had ever seen and resolved that
when the war ended, he would come back and make it his
home.

In the seventeenth century, French explorers had settled in
parts of Northern Indiana and established Catholic churches
there, cultivating fertile ground for the founding of Notre Dame
University in South Bend in 1842. Farther east, huge communities of Amish and Mennonite settlers developed, drawn by rich
and level farmland and the longing to escape discrimination
from those who were not members of their sects.

While I could have introduced the land of my birth from
numerous angles, I cannot overstate the Caucasian religious
influence in the settling of Northern Indiana, particularly the
Elkhart Prairie region. Nor can I exaggerate the virulent racism
permeating the entire state of Indiana in the 1920s when
numerous members of the State Legislature were open
members of the Ku Klux Klan and then-Governor Edward L.
Jackson (not related to Colonel John Jackson) fraternized with
D. C. Stephenson, Grand Dragon of the Indiana Klan, who
discussed with Jackson issues of interest to the Klan, such as
eliminating the influence of Roman Catholics, Jews and 'col-
oreds' (sic).[3]

Until the great migration of blacks from the South to Northern industrial centers such as Chicago, Detroit, Cleveland, St. Louis, and other urban centers in the upper Midwest, Northern Indiana remained almost exclusively white until ripples of the migration spread to South Bend. Smaller industrial cities such as Elkhart remained predominantly white until after World War II.

Into this milieu I was born in 1945. At that time, Elkhart was thriving economically as the mobile home industry had just been launched, and scores of veterans returned home from the war. My father did not serve in World War II, but he and my mother did find secure employment with the Ford Motor Company's Willow Run Airplane Manufacturing site in Ypsilanti, Michigan.

My father tirelessly proclaimed his born-again conversion at the age of sixteen, which I now understand as his lifeline to sanity and a critical buffer between himself and the excruciating pain of childhood trauma. Equally traumatized was my mother, the same age as my father, who grew up with an alcoholic father and a ghastly history of sexual abuse. Championing their conversion to Christian fundamentalism in the church they both attended, my parents inevitably found one another and married in 1939.

As an only child of two zealous fundamentalists, church, twice on Sunday and once on Wednesday evenings, with frequent revival meetings and a host of church activities added in the mix, was my life for the first eighteen years. With a bright and precocious intellect, I memorized scores of Bible verses. For reasons I don't clearly recall, at the age of four or five, I began my mornings by "preaching the gospel" in my bedroom. Soon, my father made me a wooden pulpit to encourage my fantasy ministry. Imitating my parents' overbearing compulsion to attempt to convert the "unbelievers" they encountered, I "preached," not only to the walls of my bedroom, but to everyone I met, by quoting scripture and lecturing them on the hellfire and brimstone that would be their end if they did not accept Jesus as their personal savior.

Not surprisingly, I was "preaching" before I had the born-again experience that my parents told me I must have, but that would soon be remedied. Every summer my parents attended a week-long Christian convention at Winona Lake, Indiana in the Billy Sunday Memorial Tabernacle. During my fourth summer on earth at Winona Lake, I accepted Jesus as my personal savior at the end of a Billy Graham crusade meeting. From hindsight I realize that that while my parents loved me, this born-again moment promoted me to sainthood in their eyes. For the rest of my life, I would be reminded that I had been "saved" at the age of four and that I must think, feel, and behave accordingly. From hindsight, of course, I had little idea of what "being saved" actually meant, but like any four-year-old who was a child of authoritarian parents, I submitted to the game plan. As Dr. Marlene Winell states, "A child at the age of four or five does not have a fully-developed brain, and it's crazy to believe that a child that age can embrace a religion like this... Kids conform because they need to be dependent on their parents."[4]

Yet another reality of my early childhood was that at the end of every sermon in church when the pastor invited people to walk to the front of the church and accept Jesus, very sad music was played. Hymns such as "Just As I Am" or "Almost Persuaded" or "Pass Me Not Oh Gentle Savior," almost always accompanied this "altar call," and I remember, as early as the age of 3, being overcome with tears during the altar call. When my mother asked me why I was crying, I had no idea, and I would often say, "I don't know." To this day I *don't* know with certainty, but I suspect that some part of my psyche was sad and distressed after hearing an hour of raging condemnation of sinners—the spewing of copious amounts of hell fire and brimstone vitriol by a zealous, screaming preacher. All I knew in the moment was that it hurt my heart.

Ironically, in the same year as my "conversion," my mother had an affair with her doctor, and it appeared that my parents' marriage was over. I became very ill with what was erroneously diagnosed as asthma, the doctor recommending that I be taken to a warmer climate. Meanwhile, my mother gave birth to the doctor's child, who was severely disabled and lived only five months. Subsequently, my mother, my maternal grandparents, and I moved to South Texas for nearly a year, and eventually, my parents reconciled, all the while pretending that everything was normal. Throughout my entire life until shortly before my father's passing in 2020, both my parents denied that the affair had ever taken place. Undoubtedly the most dramatic example of my parents' hypocrisy, it was only one of countless instances of professing one thing and living another. Before his death, my father finally admitted that the affair had taken place. Decades earlier I had confronted my parents about the affair, and they had insisted it had never happened and that I was stirring up trouble in the family because I had left the Christian fold.

Throughout my early childhood I was sexually abused by my mother. Children experiencing trauma and abuse frequently act out their distress, and in my ninth and tenth year, I became physically violent at school. My hitting, harassing, and tormenting my peers became uncontrollable, and my parents were warned by teachers to control me, otherwise I would be expelled and possibly institutionalized. My parents' response was to increasingly escalate physical punishment with beatings, prefaced by lengthy recitations of scripture and monumental episodes of shaming. Try as I would to control my violent impulses, I could not. The severity of the beatings intensified, and with each one, I left my body and went numb.

Miraculously and for whatever reason, I stopped acting out as I approached adolescence and grew increasingly, secretly rebellious against my parents and their religion. I ceased being violent and began engaging in behaviors which I knew they would find abhorrent. In fundamentalist circles in those days, the "Filthy Five" were axiomatic: No smoking, drinking, dancing, card-playing, or going to movies. At that point my parents were pre-occupied with business, and I had more time alone than I had ever had, which I often spent dancing and listening to fifties rock music. In the afternoons, I hurried home from school to secretly watch and dance with "American Bandstand" on television while my parents were working away from home. While I kept my cards close to the vest, my parents sensed that I was growing increasingly rebellious, and they sold their business in order to more closely surveil my activities. At that point I intuited that in terms of my survival physically and emotionally, it was "game over" if my true feelings were discovered, and I chose to dive wholeheartedly into church activities. I did not consciously understand that I was doing so in order to save my sanity and possibly my life, but surrender I did. Concurrently, I began to realize the intensity of my attraction to other females, and I also knew that acting on any of my attractions would be dangerous and devastating for me. After years of reflection on my submission to my parents' religion, I now realize that I made a sad but ultimately wise decision.

Like a caged animal, I submitted to my confinement. To do otherwise could have meant being psychologically obliterated by my parents, so I became the trained monkey in the fundamentalist circus. The cages were numerous—an organization for born-again teenagers called Youth for Christ, endless church activities, attempting to convert my adolescent peers, applying for college, but all the while, developing one crush after another on my female friends. Inside my cage I carried an enormous and deadly secret whenever I heard gossip about Christian men who were caught in bathrooms having sex with each other and women roommates who were "more than just good friends." I read every piece of Christian literature I could find on the Christian view of homosexuality. I did my own research on what the Bible said on the topic, and increasingly, I was convinced that God could deliver me from this horrific sin if I prayed hard enough and controlled my thoughts.

In 1894, the Mennonite community in Northern Indiana had established a college in the nearby city of Goshen, and I chose to attend my first year of college there because I could commute and live at home. While I was determined to attend college, my parents were reluctant to condone my leaving home, and I was well aware that I wasn't ready to leave at all. A nearby college seemed to be the perfect solution, until I realized that Goshen College was a bastion of progressive political and religious liberalism. At home I learned that Martin Luther King, Jr. was a communist and that President John Kennedy was probably the antichrist. I was pathetically racist and rabidly conservative, saving my spare change to be able to afford joining the John Birch Society. While I enjoyed most of my college classes, I read articles in the student newspaper and heard sermons in daily required chapel meetings about the heroic accomplishments of the Freedom Riders in the South and the integration of schools in Mississippi. I felt dangerously threatened by the liberalism that surrounded me, and I longed for training in theology and evangelism. The appeal of monastic isolation in a cloistered fundamentalist environment was tantalizing and stupefyingly irresistible. Thus, I applied to my church's denominational alternative to my liberal nightmare, Moody Bible Institute in Chicago.

Decades before the popularity of the saying, "If you want to make God laugh, tell Him your plans," I moved into my dorm room six blocks from Lake Michigan in an area called the Gold Coast—known for its nightlife and bohemian lifestyles. Only three blocks away was Washington Park, also known as Bughouse Square in the 1920s and 30s, where left-wing radicals of the day used to give speeches to union organizers. In more recent times, it had become a pickup area for gay men in search of sexual encounters.

One Friday afternoon as I was practicing a sermon in the speech lab, the radio loudspeaker announced that John F. Kennedy had been shot in Dallas. That evening, many of us gathered in the dorm to have a discussion about what happened. I felt strangely naïve as one woman in particular, Julie, spoke very articulately about Kennedy and what he had accomplished. For reasons still unknown to me, instead of contesting her opinion of Kennedy, I just listened, and in doing so, I began to realize that there were some aspects of Kennedy that I had missed because I was seeing his agenda too narrowly. But that would mean that I would have to think twice about my *racism*, not a word I was familiar with at the time, as well as other aspects of my political perspective.

The following week, Kennedy's funeral was televised, and Julie and I sat together sobbing into boxes of Kleenex as we watched. Why was I crying? This guy was supposed to be the antichrist. Jackie and her artsy-fartsy White House beautification had been the brunt of family jokes, and now I was feeling heartbreak for her as I watched her holding John-John's hand while he saluted his father's passing coffin with his other little hand. Suddenly, I felt myself finding a strange cultural and intellectual camaraderie with Julie and some other students in the dorm.

My first year in Bible college was intellectually mediocre and consumed with meaningless busy work that encouraged jumping through hoops. I felt academically adrift until I took a freshman English course in my second semester in which we were required to write a research paper. "Choose a topic that you don't know much about but would like to learn *more* about," the professor suggested. Increasingly curious as I had become about race, I chose to do a research paper on the topic.

Although I did not state my quest in words, it was simply to determine if "negroes" were actually human beings "like white people are human beings."

Looking back on this one paper more than fifty years later, I am compelled to acknowledge that it was a turning point in my life. After completing it, I never again questioned that people of color are human beings. While it was only the beginning of my lifelong quest to become "woke" on the topic of racism—a mere dip of the toe into the water, it changed me forever. Today I can only wonder what might happen to young people from racist backgrounds in the twenty-first century if they were taught to think critically and do such in-depth research on the topic of race.

I would end my first year of Bible college in the "worldly" Near North Side of Chicago and go back home to Indiana. A few months later, the Civil Rights Act would be passed, and my father would rant obsessively about how the n_____'s were going to take over. My mother would be particularly verbally abusive as she realized she was losing her daughter to adulthood. She insisted that I take a job in a local bakery that required me to get up at 4 AM so that I could "learn how to be responsible and hold down a job." Julie and I would write letters back and forth all summer, and I would count the days until I could see her again.

In my 2006 memoir, *Coming Out from Fundamentalist Christianity*, I recounted the story of my agonizing affair with Julie, which was doomed to end adversely due to the homophobic shame in which we were both ensnared. Near the end of the affair, I learned of a fundamentalist psychologist in the Chicago area who was only too happy to confirm my shame and assist me in "changing" and "becoming a truly feminine woman" through Christian psychotherapy. I was on the road to becoming "normal," I incessantly told myself. Only months after the relationship with Julie ended, I was again involved with another former Bible college student shortly before moving to another Midwestern state to attend university. Julie had been my motivation in choosing that school because she had grown up near the campus and was planning to attend as well. Even after our relationship came to a traumatic and ugly end, I was determined to enroll. Much of my motivation, of course, was to be near Julie, but even that pathetic desire became a gift in terms of the ultimate transformation that resulted from having a university education.

Part of the nearly-tragic ending of the relationship with Julie was my suicide attempt. I had often considered jumping to my death from the ten-story women's dorm at the college, but one night, feeling horrifically despondent and terrified about losing Julie, I went to a nearby liquor store a few blocks from campus and bought a fifth of vodka with a fake ID. I returned to the dorm and drank all of it with the intention of passing out and never waking up. My roommate later found me unconscious in my bed, and she immediately called the resident assistant for help. That woman happened to be Julie's sister, and she sensed what my suicide attempt was about. Fortunately for me, everyone who knew of the incident kept quiet about it, or I would have been expelled from Bible college then and there.

A few months later, after Julie had left me and Chicago, I was overwhelmed with guilt and visited the Dean of Women to confess the relationship. I was put on probation for a few weeks, then called into the dean's office and asked to leave the school. In addition, the Dean called my parents and shared my "disgrace" with them.

My parents demanded that I move back home, but by this time, I was eerily aware that were I to return to live with my parents, I would either end up in a mental hospital or dead. With herculean resistance, I refused to return home and chose to remain in Chicago and find a job. From hindsight I now realize that my decision was the most consequential one of my young life because it guaranteed that I would survive. Capitulating to my parents would have destroyed me. My decision was an incipient and vulnerable step in the direction of establishing and maintaining physical and emotional boundaries with my parents, but make it I did, and I have never looked back.

While at Bible college and shortly after leaving, I realized that I was not the only student being torn apart emotionally by internalized homophobia. I heard rumors about Tim, who sat in my church history class looking profoundly depressed, staring at the floor in every class, until one day he disappeared from campus and was never heard from again. The cover story was, "Tim felt called to study at another Bible college." And there was Sarah, who attempted suicide and left school abruptly, and Fran, who "needed to go home and take care of her mom." These were just three of the many students around me that were carrying the same secret I was carrying.

In moments of agitated depression and fitful anxiety, I took long walks throughout the Near North Side of Chicago to get away from campus. Many times I found myself stopping to rest at Bughouse Square, where gay men picked each other up and which became a sickening but riveting clandestine shame-fest for me. I was drawn to the secret I shared with them that, like a tragic car crash, I couldn't look at but also couldn't look away from.

I continued in therapy with the Christian psychologist for several months after leaving Moody. One evening on my long journey to the therapist's office in a distant suburb, I encountered Luke, who I recognized as a former Moody student. We rode the el together for several miles and agreed to have coffee soon. A few days later we met in a restaurant near the Moody campus, and Luke came out to me, telling me that he had to drop out before he got caught having sex with another man. He seemed to have come to terms with his sexual orientation, while I, on the other hand, was still attempting to become heterosexual. Nevertheless, we became confidants and discussed many of the other students whom we suspected were gay, Luke telling me that he believed that our Bible college was "a hothouse for homosexuality." Indeed it was, as are countless religious schools of all denominations who demand that students repress their diverse sexual orientations.

At that point in my life, the perplexity was not that I didn't become wildly heterosexual in order to "cure myself," but that I continued to embrace punitive Christianity. On the one hand, I was mentally and spiritually abandoning fundamentalism and exploring a more liberal Christian perspective, laden with the writings of sophisticated theologians, but on the other hand, I clung to my homophobic delusions about my sexual orientation. Sadly, no theologian or pastor in those days offered even a hint of acceptance of LGBTQ people.

I did enroll at the university Julie was now attending, but my attempts to connect with her were angrily thwarted. I was then forced to decide what was more important to me—forcing myself on someone who was terrified of their attraction to me, or getting an education. In my first year, I sought out a local church of a liberal denomination and proceeded to engage in intellectual discussions of the Bible and Christian theology with the pastor and other parishioners, all the while never disclosing my sexual orientation and keeping it under wraps. Now desperate to "change," I launched a personal crusade with myself to become heterosexual. I visited the student counseling center and began therapy with a kind and perceptive therapist named Grace to whom I declared in the first session that I wanted her to make me straight. In those days, homosexuality was still considered a pathology by the American Psychological Association and would be until 1973. Not only was my fundamentalist background driving my crusade to become heterosexual, but so was the disparaging information I was hearing in my psychology classes regarding homosexuality, which was also labeled a pathology in my Abnormal Psychology textbook. I now had it on "good authority," both from the Bible and from psychology, that I was sick and needed to be "cured."

Grace was compassionate and did not set out to "cure" me even though I demanded it. She suggested that I should experiment with dating men if I thought it would facilitate my desire to change. I immediately answered a couple of dating ads, which in those days operated by mail. I began dating college men and found the experiences awkward, if not absurd, yet I persisted. After a few dates I decided that I wanted to stop dating and focus all of my energy on improving my grades and sharpening my intellect—a decision that allowed me to kick the can of sexual orientation down the road a bit longer. I had been a psychology major, but despite my attraction to psychology, I chose to major in my second love, history.

The Vietnam War was escalating, as were protests and rioting by black communities in major cities throughout the country. In the process of becoming increasingly radicalized politically, I joined Students for a Democractic Society, (SDS) where I encountered only heterosexuals, most of whom avoided and mocked gay people. The women's movement was in its infancy, and even there, lesbians were treated as inferior and perverted. Feminist icon Betty Friedan referred to them as "the lavender menace."

In his later years my father blamed my sexual orientation on "those terrible things" I learned at the university. In reality, the truly "terrible" things I learned there were relics of antiquated Freudian psychology with its patriarchal, pathologizing punditry regarding human sexuality. I could never have dreamed of living an openly lesbian lifestyle as a student or having numerous LGBTQ organizations on campus to offer support—the now-unquestioned reality of twenty-first century universities.

Nevertheless, my university education greased the wheels of

my journey out of my fundamentalist prison, and I imagine that for the rest of my life, I will revisit my alma mater as often as possible, as I already have many times over the years. Every American university has made despicable deals with the devil in terms of sports programs, contracts with transnational corporations, and environmental degradation. For example, in more recent years, the university I attended was the scene of a horrific sexual abuse scandal involving a sports medicine physician and numerous female gymnasts. Yet I owe my life and my sanity to the education I received there. I love visiting the campus and quietly walking its beautiful pristine paths, stopping to listen to the babbling of the river that flows through it, and pondering the vintage buildings where I sat in large lecture halls in voracious receptivity to higher education. For me, that bucolic and serene campus will always be a sacred hospital where a part of me was born.

As I immersed myself in psychology and history classes, my faith began to disintegrate, and soon I was yet another twenty-something college student searching for the meaning of life because I was now rejecting religion entirely and ultimately identified as an atheist.

Eventually, I carried on a closeted relationship with another female student under the guise of "we're just really good friends" at a time when two inseparable women, never seen with men but only together, raised more than a few eyebrows. Increasingly, we grew emotionally distant and separated, spectacularly facilitated by the homophobia within ourselves and everyone in our world.

As with nearly every university campus in America in 1970, ours was in upheaval due to the Vietnam War and the cultural revolution of the moment. My atheism grew more entrenched as the bitterness and despair of the sixties raged but eventually congealed into a new iteration of individualism. Marijuana and I were old friends, but I had never indulged in psychedelics. On a balmy April night a group of friends invited me to partake, and I would never be the same. My atheist adult succumbed to the childhood hunger for God that had never left me, and I was launched into a search for ultimate truths that has endured for more than five decades. Yet I soon realized the limits of psychedelics in the spiritual journey they enabled me to embrace.

After graduation from university, I moved back to Chicago briefly and once again lived on the Near North Side. While I was now adrift but searching, mostly unemployed and uncertain of my future, I noticed an ad in a feminist newspaper with the headline, "Radical Lesbians Invite You To Come Out." I had never spoken the word "lesbian" in my life, but I was haunted by the ad and decided to investigate. On a dark, brutally cold winter night in Chicago, I ventured south to a neighborhood near the University of Chicago and entered a basement apartment in abject terror. The room was packed with lesbians who greeted me warmly and invited me to share. I somehow found words to say that I was anxious, dismayed, and feeling terminally alone with my "secret." The meeting lasted nearly two hours, and I was both disoriented and euphoric as the women invited me to join them at a women's bar. Little did I know that the bar was located on my way back to the Near North Side, but only two blocks from my former Bible college. At the bar I felt that I had come home to a place I had never left yet at the same time, I was stunned with the realization of what this would mean for me going forward.

I continued to attend Radical Lesbian meetings and cultivate my feminist consciousness. No longer was I bored and adrift. I felt ready to launch my life alongside the spiritual journey I had recently embraced. Just as I had grasped the limits of ingesting psychedelics, I clearly realized the limits of the Midwest as my horizons expanded, and a trip to Colorado compelled me to move there.

Soon after arriving in Colorado I fell in love and entered a relationship with a woman with a troubled past who had also been raised in fundamentalism and who, like me, had thoroughly rejected it. But this relationship did not happen in the closet. I had thoroughly come out to myself, and in our small town of Colorado Springs, we met at a gay bar named The Hide and Seek. During this time, I also began a daily meditation practice that helped center me and assisted me in weathering the storm of my partner's untimely death at the age of 27 from a drug overdose. Her passing was the first encounter with death so personally and so intimately in my life.

Then, after six years in Colorado and a Master's degree in hand, I moved west because, like so many millions of LGBTQ people in those days, who would not welcome the opportunity to live in a less homophobic milieu? Landing in Laguna Beach, the LGBTQ mecca of Southern California, I felt free for the first time in my life.

In the euphoria of my liberation I began attending Science of Mind and Unity churches. Their emphasis on positive thinking and unconditional love were irresistible. After a lifetime of being battered by the doctrine of original sin, the notion of original perfection was a balm for my soul and body. Was this really heaven on Earth? I could be an out lesbian with a positive spiritual path free of shame, judgment, and the threat of hell fire and brimstone. LGBTQ groups were ubiquitous in Southern California, and soon I was dating Darlene, with whom I would spend the next 11 years. Our relationship felt solid as we developed our careers in Southern California, but our travels to Northern California raised another possibility—living in a less congested and even more accepting area of the state.

We were both in therapy, and I was now in a Master's in Counseling program with plans to become a psychotherapist. Choosing to move to the North Bay Area would position us in a more rural area amid a large lesbian community with unimaginable opportunities for personal and spiritual development, just an hour north of San Francisco, the focal point of LGBTQ energy in the country. What could possibly go wrong?

Shortly after the move, "trouble in paradise" rocked our relationship as I became increasingly disagreeable to live with. I entered therapy again, this time with a woman trained in Jungian therapy. Not being specifically familiar with Jung, but now uncovering physical, sexual, emotional, and spiritual abuse in my childhood, I was riveted, but also ripped open to an aspect of my quest for meaning and purpose that I could never have imagined. I was introduced to the concept of "the shadow" with which I was completely unfamiliar—at least intellectually. In fact, the shadow had permeated my life, coloring every inch of the religion I had been indoctrinated with. My fundamentalist notions of "love" were marinated in hate, arrogance, prejudice, and violence. The touting of "moral purity" was the window dressing that disguised sexual abuse, adultery, lust, greed, and betrayal.

Jungian therapy for me was a shattering experience because it exposed the malevolence of my upbringing, but it was also deeply alluring because it was the *truth*. Fundamentalist Christianity with its authoritarian hypocrisy was not real. New Age spirituality with its positive thinking obsession and spiritual bypassing was not real. What *was* real? The essence of who I am with all of my wounding and shadowy defects of character and infinite networks of vulnerability. The inner work drew me to myth, symbolism, and my imagination. I was now able to think with complexity and nuance, rather than simplistically, with a binary, black and white mindset. At the same time, the narrow corridors of my industrially civilized Western upbringing were giving way to vistas of fascination with indigenous cultures and their wisdom.

My encounter with Jung in the therapeutic container lasted 11 years and impacted every aspect of my life. Darlene and I increasingly grew in different directions, and I left California and my own therapy practice to relocate in New Mexico, and later back to Colorado.

By the 1980s, I had minimal contact with my parents, who were horrified that I had left the Midwest and were aghast that I was living in California. Visits with them were sparse, but about the time I had moved to California, I noticed dramatic changes in their religious behavior. They abandoned their fundamentalist Baptist church and fell head over heels into Pentecostalism, touting their baptism with the Holy Spirit. They began dressing like eighties televangelists and attending Pentecostal workshops and conferences around the country. We never spoke openly about my being gay, but I sensed that my move to California, my relaxed lesbian appearance, and the reality of a significant other in my life had driven them into an extreme iteration of fundamentalism. They had no heterosexual children to adore for their heterosexuality, nor any grandchildren. In fact, they had no other children at all.

In the few conversations I did have with my parents in those days, they frequently mentioned their ability to cast out demons as a result of having received the baptism of the Holy Spirit. They freely opined that people who used drugs or had sex outside of marriage, and especially those who had contracted HIV, were demon-possessed. My father penned volumes of sermonizing letters with extensive citations of scripture to me and would frequently send books about the Rapture and the end times that I never read but immediately tossed in the trash. Occasionally, I would receive phone calls from a Pentecostal cohort of my parents who "just happened to be in the area" and would like to have lunch with me. Another strategy, of course, to suck me in. Sometimes I accepted the invitation, only to find myself bombarded with attempts to bring me back to the Christian fold. Eventually, I shored up my boundaries and refused any invitations from friends of my parents, which were simply the tentacles of my parents extended through other people.

While neither of my parents ever accused me of being "demon-possessed," I am well aware of their belief that gay people carried the "demon" of homosexuality. When I first realized their belief—that I was at the very least "demon-influenced"—it was a brutal psychological blow that felt as if I had literally been hit with a fist. It was the ultimate "othering"—a wall of rejection that felt insurmountable because it was. Eventually, as I learned more about the wounding of each of my parents, I felt less battered and humiliated by their belief and began to feel compassion for them because they were incapable of accepting same-gender attraction in anyone, let alone their daughter.

Whereas I could speak with my mother on other topics besides religion until she passed in 2003, it was impossible to maintain a conversation with my dad without his attempting to convert me. However, his proselytizing efforts were not unique to me. Everyone who knew him felt the need to dodge the bullets of his sermonizing. Throughout his life this meant that nonfundamentalists tended to avoid him if possible, leaving him with only his fundamentalist friends, whom he clearly preferred. When forced to interact with an accountant, attorney, or other professional, he preferred only those who fit his definition of "Christian."

In another memoir written in 2018, I recounted my reconnection with my father after a long period of estrangement for the purpose of securing long-term care for him. During the last four years of his life, every encounter by phone or in person would invariably include some attempt to convert me. On some occasions it was necessary to firmly assert my boundaries, at best, and to unequivocally terminate the conversation, at worst.

I disclosed very little of my life to my father as an adult. I learned early on that doing so would result in protracted campaigns to set me straight and bring the "Prodigal Daughter" back to the fold. At the end of his life, he knew perhaps ten percent of who I am, and that is a generous estimate. Every interaction with him required me to be "on guard"—ready to quickly erect impenetrable boundaries in order to protect my emotional and spiritual space. My relationship with my father required me to be a psychological contortionist: Staying a step ahead of him in hiding most of who I was, while quickly constructing concrete barriers between us to protect myself from the spiritual assaults of his missionary zeal.

My father passed at the age of 102, but he was lucid and largely cognitively intact to the end. One of the gifts of his long life to me was a series of stories he told about his own childhood. As a former therapist and someone who has been in long-term therapy myself, it is clear to me that he was emotionally and sexually abused. Various forms of abuse were also part of my mother's story, and as is so often the case, my parents found and stabilized each other in the context of a fundamentalist Christian church without ever acknowledging their wounding.

I mourn for myself, but also for my father. Abraham Piper, "exvangelical" Prodigal Son of prominent Christian author John Piper, asks, "Do you know how boring and soul-sucking it is to base your whole life on making sure other people change to become more like you?"[5] My father's life was consumed with that soul-sucking obsession, and I can only wonder who he might have been without it.

Even after decades of therapy, receiving the support of trusted friends, and creating a life for which I am profoundly grateful as I grapple with aging, the post-traumatic stress of my childhood fundamentalist upbringing is with me. I recognize it in my anxiety, a tendency to catastrophize, the low-grade PTSD-rage that boils in my belly, and occasional regrets that I missed experiencing a "normal" childhood. Nevertheless, I feel deep peace with myself and the divine within me. Perhaps the best way to describe my spiritual path these days comes from the title of a book written by a fellow recovering fundamentalist ally, Frank Schaeffer. I am "an atheist who believes in God."[6] That is to say, the "God" that most atheists don't believe in is the "God" I don't believe in.

With deep gratitude to Jung and to the world of myth, story, poetry, symbolism, archetypes, and images, I increasingly crave the gifts of the right brain and the soul. The left-brain world of doctrine and theology no longer serve me. As I continue to cherish the blessings of both the right and left brain, I become less drawn to intellectual knowing and more enchanted with the soul's wisdom. For many years I have been a student of the Perennial Tradition, which is not a sect or denomination, but a treasure trove of universal wisdom. One of my most respected spiritual teachers, Franciscan Father Richard Rohr, speaking of the Perennial Tradition, writes:

> The Perennial Tradition points to recurring themes and truths within all of the world's religions. At their most mature level, religions cultivate in their followers a deeper union with God, with each other, and with reality—or *what is*. The work of religion is *re-ligio*—re-ligament or reunion with what our egos and survival instincts have put asunder, namely a fundamental wholeness at the heart of everything. [7]

I have come to believe that evangelicals do not comprehend what they are reading when they read: "I turned my heart to know and to search out and to seek wisdom and the scheme of things." (Ecclesiastes 7:25) Because fundamentalist Christianity is so thoroughly obsessed with "knowing," there is little room for appreciating or savoring wisdom. Wisdom is not acquired through knowledge or intellect but through the soul. The soul is the crux of our humanity, and all fundamentalists acknowledge that fact, but they view the soul as something that must be "saved," rather than the mirror image of the divine within us that we did not acquire and that we cannot "lose."

As Rabbi Rami Shapiro writes in the *World Wisdom Bible*, "truth is that which collapses the divisions between chosen and not chosen, believer and infidel, saved and damned, and leads to the understanding that we are all one community of seekers."[8] Shapiro summarizes Perennial Wisdom as:

1. All life arises in and is an expression of the non-dual Infinite Life that is called by many names: Ultimate Reality, God, Tao, Mother, Allah, YHVH, Dharmakaya, Brahma, and Great Spirit, among others.

2. You contain two ways of knowing the world: a greater knowing (called Atman, Soul, Self, Spirit, or Mind, along with a host of other names) that intuitively knows each finite life as a unique manifestation of Infinite Life, and a lesser knowing (called self, ego, *aham*, *kibr*, and the like) that mistakes uniqueness for separateness and imagines itself apart from, rather than a part of Infinite Life.

3. Awakening the Self and knowing the interconnectedness of all life in the singular Life carries with it a universal ethic calling the awakened to cultivate compassion and justice toward all beings.

4. Awakening your Self and living this ethic is the highest goal you can set for yourself.[9]

"Religions are like languages," Shapiro writes. Each religion speaks to a different facet of our experience. Our sense of reality can be broadened, of course, if we learn many languages. "Just as being born into a mother tongue does not preclude you from speaking other languages, so being born into a specific religion or no religion at all does not preclude you from learning the wisdom of any and all religions. And just as the more languages you know the more nuanced your understanding of life becomes, so the more religions you know the more nuanced your understanding of Truth becomes."[10]

For the past 42 years I have embraced a daily meditation practice. It is a source of profound serenity and grounding, and at the same time, another intimate connection with the sacred. I am blessed to live close to the Rocky Mountains with easy access to wild nature. Here I daily discover, in the words of poet Wendell Berry, "the peace of wild things." In recent years, wild nature has profoundly shaped my spirituality—so much so that I find it almost impossible to sit in a church service without longing to be wandering in nature, communing with plants, animals, birds, the soil, the sky, the rivers and streams.

While I appreciate and clearly owe my life to my higher education journey, which will continue for the rest of my life, I am equally grateful I could expand my perspective beyond scientific materialism. Deep engagement with the wisdom of Jung, archetypal psychology, indigenous cosmology, mythology, poetry, art, and music have enlivened and embodied my rational, linear orientation with quantum reality and the art and science of consciousness. This is not a dissociated world of imaginary Biblical friends or the slavish pursuit of "God's will for my life," but rather a larger, inclusive perspective that holds the realities of two different worlds of knowing and being in the world.

In 2018, when visiting a friend at a long-term care facility not far from where I live, I encountered Grace—yes, my therapist at the university I attended. Then in her nineties, but amazingly lucid, we discussed our client-therapist relationship at the university counseling center all those years ago. She was thrilled that I had come out and was now comfortable with my sexual orientation, telling me that she wished me only loving relationships for the rest of my life. Our time together was deeply touching and rewarding, and it was one of many pieces of my history that had come full circle.

Shortly before his death in 2020 I told my dad that the most important gift he ever gave me, besides life itself, was my university education. He wasn't able to receive my appreciation because he believed that it "ruined" me. But I didn't need him to understand; I just needed to thank him.

REVOLUTIONARY REPENTANCE

Evangelicals generally define *repentance* as "changing one's mind" or abandoning one's way of life and embracing another. The Century Dictionary defines repentance as "a change of mental and spiritual attitude toward sin." In rejecting fundamentalist Christianity, I believe that I have "repented" in a way that eludes fundamentalism, because I have experienced a change in my mental and spiritual *attitude* toward sin. Rather than viewing myself as "originally sinful," I have embraced the theological perspective of "original blessing." I no longer embrace the fall/redemption perspective that assumes that humans are "fallen" creatures that must be redeemed.

Original sin was neither a Jewish concept nor a first-century Christian one. It arose with Augustine and other church fathers. As former Catholic theologian Matthew Fox wrote in *Original Blessing*, "Augustine mixed his doctrine of original sin up with his peculiar notions about sexuality."[11] Augustine was consumed with shame regarding his own sexuality—so consumed that his personal baggage about sexuality dictated his theology. What is more, even though not all church fathers embraced the doctrine of original sin, the doctrine proved advantageous for the church and its missionary efforts, because if humans are originally sinful and in need of redemption, they need look no further than the church to absolve their sin. In other words, the original sin doctrine became an ingenious marketing tool for the church and continues to benefit fundamentalist Christianity exponentially as the threat of "the end times" and the Rapture intensifies.

The "good news" of the gospel was and is the compassion, interconnectedness, forgiveness, and unconditional love that

Jesus taught, not the original sinfulness, shame, worthlessness, and separation that the church fathers, the Roman Catholic Church, the leaders of the Protestant Reformation and fundamentalist Christianity have proclaimed in both ancient and modern times. So yes, I have repented. I have abandoned the notion that I am separate from God, from other humans, and from the earth. I have embraced my sexuality and my sexual orientation, recalling that Jesus never said a word about sexual orientation and that the Apostle Paul and other apostles and church fathers wrote their homophobic diatribes on sexual orientation because they were threatened by their own sexuality and that of others, particularly women.

While writing this book in 2021, Dr. Paul Maxwell, a Ph.D. student at Trinity Evangelical Divinity School, and philosophy professor at Moody Bible Institute, released a video in which he tearfully announced that he is no longer a Christian. As I watched and listened to his remarks, I was poignantly reminded of the same tender feelings I had in the moment that I realized that I could no longer identify as a Christian. I believe that my transition was more gradual than Maxwell's, but no less traumatic. In fact, Maxwell has written a book entitled *The Trauma of Doctrine*, in which he uses the term Trauma-Induced Apostasy (TIA), apostasy meaning abandonment, rejection, and disaffection from a religious belief. Maxwell states:

> Much in the same way that those who have suffered physical trauma have certain bodily handicaps, abuse survivors bring certain emotional, relational, behavioral, and spiritual handicaps which are treated in this world as high-handed sin rather than complicated suffering. Whether these handicaps manifest themselves in sexual compulsion, drug addiction, emotional dysregulation, relational turmoil, or various other more serious psychiatric conditions, they are interpreted through the lens of obedience and disobedience, rather than

post-traumatic symptomatology. Consequently, the solution to these manifestations is instinctive *rebuke* rather than *recovery*.[12]

I believe that the very notion of original sin is traumatizing, and in many cases, intentionally so. It is a form of spiritual abuse inflicted on believers and non-believers alike out of emotional insecurity and a compulsion to shame, dominate, control, and manipulate the unconverted into a born-again experience and the converted into submission to specific theological or doctrinal perspectives and behaviors.

For those of us born into or converted to Christian fundamentalism, shame is our default position. We learn to mercilessly shame ourselves and to subtly or blatantly shame others in our relationships. If we actively embrace fundamentalist theology, we simply cannot hear the tender but emphatic words of Jesus commanding us to live with empathy, love, compassion, forgiveness and at the same time, to take a stand against hypocrisy and mean-spirited authority. Instead, we demand the punitive pontifications of the Apostle Paul or the ferocious diatribes of Old Testament patriarchs and their "thou shalt not's."

Indeed, as Carl Jung so painstakingly articulated, all humans possess a shadow aspect in the psyche, but the shadow is a direct result of being shamed and deciding early-on in life to disown or send away parts of the self that are not acceptable to parents or other authority figures. The Christian fundamentalist lifestyle is an onerous, colossal campaign of disowning the parts of oneself that are deemed evil, unbiblical, or not Christ-like. A booming evangelical growth industry centers around sermons, books, videos, and televangelism series on how to cast out one's personal demons and resist all manner of temptation to commit sin. Are we then surprised when a televangelist like Jimmy Swaggart is found cavorting with a prostitute or Jerry Falwell, Jr. is photographed in his underwear with a young woman less than half his age and openly admits that he loves to watch his wife having sex with another man?

In "Growing Up Evangelical," many parts of me did not grow up at all. It took facing my own shadow mercifully, with the support of others to whom I mattered, and learning to have compassion for the beautiful but broken human being that I am so that I could grow into the person I came here to be. As I continue to age, I hold regrets. Who would I have become had I not grown up in an evangelical home? What would it have been like to have parents who understood the importance of an education rather than just dutifully paying for me to have one? And while very few LGBTQ people in my generation were able to come out to parents while living at home, what would it have been like for me to be able to do so as an adult and be accepted anyway?

Of the regrets I have, none of them include regretting my "Revolutionary Repentance." In the evangelical world, much is said about grace. Some have created an acronym from the word —God's Riches at Christ's Expense. Some define grace as God's unmerited favor in the salvation of sinners. I prefer this quote from an unknown source:

Grace means that all of your mistakes now serve a purpose instead of serving shame.

Perhaps the purest embodiment of "grace" was a compassionate counselor named Grace who accepted me as I was and had no need to change me.

7. HEALING THE EVANGELICAL WOUND: RESTORING THE SOUL

To heal means to make whole, and when we feel whole, we are in touch with the whole world.
—Michael Meade, author, mythologist~[1]

"I'd be adrift in an ocean of uncertainty." Yes, and perhaps that's the only honest place to be. Another name for uncertainty is humility. No one ever blew up a mosque, church, or abortion clinic after yelling, "I could be wrong."
—Frank Schaeffer, *Sex, Mom, and God: How the Bible's Strange Take on Sex Led to Crazy Politics—and How I Learned to Love Women (and Jesus) Anyway*

But the experience of leaving can also be liberating, like breaking out of prison. If you feel oppressed by all the formulas and judgments, the rules and regulations, you might now feel a great relief, able to think and feel and experience much more of yourself. Some people describe a wonderful, almost euphoric, feeling of "coming home" when they settle in to the notion of just being alive and living life now, in this world.
—Marlene Winell, *Leaving the Fold: A Guide for Former Fundamentalists and Others Leaving Their Religion*

If you are reading this book, you are either not an evangelical Christian, you are a former evangelical who has already moved beyond the evangelical worldview, or you are an evangelical who is beginning to question your spiritual path. If you relate to the last two categories, you are not only dealing with your religious and spiritual views, you have almost certainly been traumatized. It is primarily to you that this chapter is addressed, and throughout this chapter, I will use "you" to address the reader who has experienced religious, particularly Christian fundamentalist, trauma.

If you have read the previous chapter, you know that I am not an atheist. I have a spiritual path, and I am in relationship with something greater than my own human ego, but many people who are in one of the many stages of moving beyond the evangelical perspective are deconstructing old concepts even as they are developing a new worldview. Thus, I want to clarify that when I speak of religious abuse or religious trauma, I am not disparaging spirituality or functional religion grounded in a humanistic, democratic perspective that emphasizes empathy, compassion, agency, healthy boundaries, and racial and gender inclusivity—and I do recognize that some religions and religious practices fit this description. However, in order to claim a spiritual path that nourishes all parts of you, you may need to do an enormous amount of deconstruction before you can reconstruct a path that feeds your soul.

Above all, it is crucial that you deconstruct and reconstruct from a place of extraordinary compassion for yourself.

Dr. Marlene Winell, mentioned above, is a psychologist in private practice who was raised in an evangelical, specifically Pentecostal, missionary family and specializes in assisting people in recovering from religious trauma. She is the author of *Leaving the Fold: A Guide for Former Fundamentalists and Others*

Leaving their Religion. Regarding recovery from religious trauma, Winell states:

> The effects of authoritarian religious training can last a long time and run deep, seriously impacting your ability to enjoy life. Often people have intense feelings and are not sure about how to move forward with a new framework for living. A person knowledgeable in human development can guide you through steps to rebuild your life and strengthen areas of personal development.[2]

THE FUNDAMENTALIST ABUSE CYCLE

In the Christian fundamentalist milieu, you are "stuck" with being in the world which is seen as the domain of Satan. You are encouraged to try to survive it in any way possible, especially by trying to save other people. You are told that this life is just a blink in time, and you don't know how to enjoy it, but that doesn't matter. From the fundamentalist perspective, it doesn't matter if you understand what it means to be human or not because being human is an inferior state that will be improved by accepting Jesus Christ as your personal savior, which assures that you will become perfect after you die and arrive in heaven. In summary, to recover from religious trauma is a massive endeavor because you must take apart and then reconstruct your entire worldview.

As I have related above, I left my home at the age of seventeen in a state of delayed development, having left the cocoon of being an only child, hovered over by fundamentalist parents who were trying to cope with their own wounding as well as obsessing about whether I would remain a faithful Christian after leaving their influence and launching my own life. I was steeped in teachings regarding "spiritual warfare," based on the notion that the world is the enemy, and I have to cope with its temptations by using scripture, prayer, and Christian friends to help me "overcome the world." On top of that layer of dysfunction, I was struggling with my sexual orientation, which was absolutely anathema to my religion.

Marlene Winell emphasizes that the range of the severity of religious trauma lies on a continuum. Each situation is different, based on the intensity of the traumatic experience. In some instances, religious trauma is actually a form of terrorism, as I pointed out above, because in terrorism a person faces a life-threatening situation, but they are in a helpless position. Teaching a child about the punishment of hell or even the supposedly glorious drama of the Rapture can be a form of terrorism.

In his *Slate Magazine* article, "Vanished from the Earth," Joshua Rivera states that, "As an evangelical kid, I was terrified of the rapture—and so was everyone I knew. Years after I left the faith, I wanted to understand the power it held over us all." Rivera summarizes beautifully two of the psychological impacts of growing up in a fundamentalist Christian family:

For many rapture-believing evangelicals in America, life is bookended by twin traumas. First you are welcomed with what someone endured on your behalf: Christ on the cross, bearing your sins and mine. The wrongs you have committed and the mistakes you have yet to make, all piled on a back bloodied with lashes long before it was nailed to a tree. You are going to mess up, to live a life not worthy of heaven, and therefore Jesus had to die, to right the moral balance and give you the chance to be with him in eternity.

Then you must confront the trauma that lies at the end of your own mortality. You get asked the question that can haunt you your whole life: Are you saved? If you are, great. Your walk toward heaven begins. If you aren't, damnation is always there, waiting to swallow you up should you meet an untimely end or find yourself excluded from the church's supernatural escape.[3]

Therefore, walking away from any fundamentalist worldview is not just a matter of flipping an intellectual switch; it requires deep emotional healing. If the emotional wounds are not attended to, they can have serious psychological consequences. For some, recovering from Christian fundamentalism is not unlike returning from a war with Post-Traumatic Stress Disorder.

According to Winell's assessment of religious trauma, not only have some or many evangelicals experienced various forms of abuse, but they are in relationship with an abusive deity. God is "punishing" you, and you need to monitor your every thought and deed, but you are nevertheless expected to love Him. "If you think of God as an entity," says Winell, "this is an abusive relationship." You have to first of all acknowledge that you're bad and in need of saving, and in order to forgive you, God had to send his son to Earth to die. It's as if you needed crucifixion in order to have a right to exist and certainly in order to have the right to go to heaven when you die. God had to die because you're so terrible, and you should be killed. You can only escape hell if you accept this atonement package and be hugely grateful, and you have to conform to the lifestyle that's prescribed. Salvation is not a free deal at all. Church leaders will tell you in no uncertain terms what conformity means and shame you if you do not conform. Because you are human, you are set up to sin, and this sets up a shame cycle, and that shame cycle dictates that you must come back to God, confess your sins, rededicate yourself, and God graciously accepts you back, at which point, you have the exhilaration of being accepted again. Winell also emphasizes that this is a classic abuse cycle which frequently necessitates treatment for anxiety and depression.[4]

STEPS TO HEALING AND RECOVERY

Just as we see in Twelve-Step programs for recovery from alcoholism, drug addiction, sexual addiction, codependency, and other self-destructive compulsions, recovery from religious trauma is a process, and one that requires patience, compassion, and robust support over time. Depending on the severity of the trauma, it can take many years.

As stated above, after leaving home more than fifty years ago, I am still recovering, and while I experience myself as a liberated, whole, reasonably fulfilled human being with healthy boundaries, I have moments in which I am aware that the trauma of my upbringing is still with me. On one level, I am still recovering. Yet, like many people in other recovery programs, I am grateful for the life experiences resulting from my upbringing—for the people who have supported me, for the healing I have experienced, the wisdom I have acquired, the meaning I have made of my life and the lives of other people where I have made a difference. As you enter the journey of recovery, remember that the journey is the point—not some destination that a traumatized part of you has decided you must achieve.

EDUCATE YOURSELF, LEARN TO THINK CRITICALLY

Marlene Winell states that the beginning of the end of her journey out of fundamentalism was a thorough study of the Bible. I vigorously support Bible research for people recovering from fundamentalism—but not if they only use resources provided by fundamentalist scholars. The research of archaelogists, religious historians, and non-sectarian and secular Biblical scholars is vital. I also recommend classes in comparative religion. Two scholars whose research I value are Bart Ehrman, Professor of Religious Studies at the University of North

Carolina, and Elaine Pagels, Professor of Religion at Princeton University. Widening one's perspective on the origins of the Bible and its contents is foundational in recovering from its strictly literal interpretation and the staggering confusion that can result from it.

Often, when people begin moving beyond fundamentalism, they need to learn how to think, because they have abdicated their ability to think for themselves. In order to be a functional adult human being, it is necessary to ask questions and think critically. Therefore, it is important to learn the *skill* of critical thinking. When we think critically, we are not assuming that something is true or false, good or bad because the Bible or a religious group declares it so. Instead, we ask questions about the basic assumptions on which we have based a certain belief or position. Recall my first term paper on racism mentioned above, written for an English class at the Bible college I attended, and how profoundly writing the paper changed my perspective on the topic.

The human brain has two hemispheres—the left and right. The left hemisphere or left brain is the thinking, reasoning, questioning function of the brain. The right brain is the intuitive, imaginal, instinctive, and creative function of the brain. Fundamentalism does not allow us to fully utilize either side of the brain. We cannot think critically because we assume that the Bible and our religious and theological doctrines are infallible. Likewise, we are suspicious of our intuitive, instinctive, and creative capacities as well. If our intuition is giving us important messages, we may discount or judge them because we are told that Satan is influencing us or that the only way to know what is true and how to act is with God's guidance.

An aspect of the human psyche that is depicted in myth, story, poetry, art, music, and literature is the symbolic function. Early humans thought in symbols and pictures before they developed language. Carl Jung was a pioneer in teaching the importance of intuition and symbolism in the functioning of whole, fully-developed, and creative human beings. His research proved how much humans benefit from stories, myths, and symbols. In fundamentalism, these are considered dangerous or sometimes demonic. For example, children can greatly benefit mentally and emotionally from the imagery in the Harry Potter Series, but fundamentalism considers the series evil and dangerous, and fundamentalist parents over-whelmingly forbid their children to read it.

One of the great gifts of mythology is that it can help us appreciate paradox. One mythologist, Michael Meade, states that myths are "a series of lies that communicate truth." That statement in itself is paradoxical. For example, a story may not have actually happened, but the symbols, images, lessons, and emotions the story evokes can assist us in appreciating paradox, which is a situation in which two things that seem opposite and appear to contradict each other are actually reconcilable. Or, if we cannot reconcile them in the moment, we can grapple with the apparent contradiction. When we are able to appreciate paradox, we find ourselves being able to hold in our hearts and minds different realities that seem contradictory. Fundamental-ism, however, was birthed in binary, either-or, black and white, polarized thinking, as opposed to complex, full spectrum think-ing. When people are recovering from fundamentalism, they must learn to think inclusively and holistically.

When engaging with myth, story, poetry, art, music, and literature, it is important to recognize that all are right-brain activities that can deeply enrich us and do not necessarily mean that we are not living in fact-based reality. In fact, reading and appreciating a myth and understanding that it is not factually true does not damage our mental health, but reading Biblical myths which we are forced to accept as absolutely factual can be very damaging to our mental health.

PSYCHOTHERAPY AND SUPPORT GROUPS

I also strongly suggest working with a psychotherapist who is trained in trauma recovery. The emotional repercussions of leaving fundamentalism are too painful and confusing to cope with alone. Numerous online support groups for people recovering from religious trauma and spiritual abuse are available. Anyone can join Marlene Winell's "Journey Free" online support group.[5] Another organization, Recovering from Religion, is a clearing house for a number of related support groups.
[6]

VALUE YOUR HUMANITY

As noted above, Christian fundamentalism views our existence on earth as a hostage situation in which we came here for no other reasons than to have a born-again experience and to save as many souls as possible. Consequently, we must endure our divinely appointed status by "being in the world but not of it," (John 15:19) We aren't here by any choice of our own, and after we accept Jesus as our personal savior, we must live here, but we do everything within our power not to be part of the human condition. In fact, we should overcome the human condition as much as possible. From that perspective, it is almost impossible to honor and respect our humanity or appreciate the fullness of being human with all of its nuances. Literature, art, music, and creative expressions throughout time have lamented, as well as celebrated, the full spectrum of the human condition, but these expressions are minimized at best or mocked at worst by fundamentalists who have no interest in appreciating the vicissitudes of our humanity. The fundamentalist worldview asserts that it has all of the answers to human dilemmas and that if one is a born-again Christian, they will have the answers as well. Christians are somehow "above it all" and are entitled to hold a certain arrogance about humanity.

Recovering from religious trauma requires us to deepen our *humility* regarding our *humanity*—both words originating from the world *humus* or earth. Being human means being vulnerable, and any arrogance we have about being above the human condition is unfounded, and from my perspective, abusive and disrespectful of oneself and others. At the same time that we need to deepen our humility in relation to being human, we must also practice self-compassion and nurture our self-esteem.

CATCHING UP CULTURALLY

I was not allowed to see movies as a child, and I saw my first movie in 1965—*My Fair Lady*, followed by *The Sound of Music*. Today, movies and theater are a treasured part of my life. People recovering from religious trauma can nurture their hearts and minds with the arts, with classical and secular music, and with poetry. Allow yourself to read some of the great works of literature in which people lament, love, protest, celebrate, hate, and express ambivalence about the realities of being human. I encourage you to read and watch plays and enjoy movies. For me, being able to appreciate my culture and discuss it with others is deeply satisfying and life-affirming. It validates my participation in the human story and strengthens my sense of awe regarding the creative capacities of humans.

VALUING THE BODY

Of all that is devalued in fundamentalism, nothing is devalued more than the human body. Modern research on trauma has revealed the profound and far-reaching impacts of trauma on the body and the brain. Paul in I Corinthians 9:27 said, "But I keep under my body, and bring *it* into subjection: lest that by any means, when I have preached to others, I myself should be a castaway." (KJV) In the language of the King James Version, "keep under my body" simply means that the body is "kept under" or suppressed, restrained, and tamed. From Paul to the church fathers to the twenty-first-century televangelists, the body is a source of evil, lust, greed, laziness, gluttony, and all manner of sin. Fundamentalist Christians who buy into the body's inherent evil discount the positive functioning of the body as well as the vulnerability of the body to trauma. In addition, all religious trauma is complicated and intensified if there has been physical or sexual abuse. What is more, fundamentalist teachings about the body facilitate mind-body splitting, in which people ignore the body or unconsciously send information from the body away from their consciousness. It is not unusual for people who have spent years or perhaps a lifetime in fundamentalism to unconsciously store painful, or even pleasurable, emotions deep in the body, becoming numb to them. Humans store trauma in the nervous system, and long after a traumatic experience occurs, the nervous system can be triggered by it.

Therefore, it is important to become aware of what triggers from the fundamentalist experience we are vulnerable to. Some of us can be triggered by Christian hymns or religious music or by something as simple as getting up on Sunday morning and remembering times when our most important Sunday function was church. Others might be triggered by the smell of incense or the sound of church bells.

I am particularly triggered by hymns and the religious music of my childhood. I sang in the church choir and studied sacred music in classes in Bible college. I have a somewhat schizophrenic relationship with hymns because, on the one hand, they can evoke pleasant memories of singing and worshipping with family and friends, but they also take me back to the pain of living with the secret of my sexual orientation as a teenager and young adult.

In recovering from religious trauma, the body, as well as the mind and emotions, needs recovery. This is not as simple as going for a run or working out at the gym. Body healing can be facilitated by working with a psychotherapist as well as people who are specifically trained to help us access and heal trauma in the body. To reiterate, simply changing your thinking is not enough for recovery.

Kindness toward and care for the body is a necessary aspect of recovery. Whereas words like these may be misunderstood as selfishness, slothfulness, self-centeredness, or as failure to "mortify the flesh," people recovering from religious trauma must develop a new relationship with the body based on compassion and care. Learning more about anatomy and physiology and the actual scientific realities of the body may enhance appreciation for the miracle that the body actually is. Something as simple as learning about the human eye and how it functions can evoke a sense of awe for the complexity, mystery, and innately flawless calculations the body makes in its functioning from moment to moment.

DEVELOPING EMPATHY FOR SUFFERING

As noted above, fundamentalism instills a sense of arrogance in the "saved" regarding the "unsaved." Often, what looks like compassion such as "a burden for the lost" or "a passion to save souls" is not compassion at all, but yet another form of religious arrogance. In many fundamentalist churches, little compassion for the poor, homeless, and disabled exists. Sometimes these churches teach that people are poor because they aren't born again or they aren't tithing or they are lazy. Disability may be considered a punishment for rejecting Jesus. The assumption is that if one is white, born again, and following Jesus and the church to the letter, these "trials and tribulations" will not befall them.

As noted above, fundamentalism tends to de-emphasize the teachings of Jesus regarding compassion, empathy, and real-world service to those who are suffering unless one is going to attempt to save their souls. In other words, "service" may not be service at all but rather a manipulation to entice people to accept Jesus as their personal savior. I encourage people in religious recovery to read the Gospels of Matthew, Mark, and Luke and notice above all the way Jesus related to common, suffering, hurting, humans. Nowhere does he say, "If you just accept me as your personal savior, everything will get better" or "you are suffering because you aren't 'saved.'" Without condition, without manipulation, he heals, supports, and comforts the sick, the poor, and the outcasts. At the same time, he rebukes those who have caused their suffering and those who continue to profit from it.

I believe that every Caucasian on earth needs to confront their culturally-programmed racism. As cited above in the work of Robert Jones, fundamentalist Christians are some of the most blatantly racist people in America. It is as if they have never read the teachings of Jesus and have no empathy toward anyone who is not white. Recovering from fundamentalism requires humility, compassion, and empathy toward, in the words of Jesus, "the least of these" because at any moment, any of us can become "the least of these."

At some point in our recovery from fundamentalism, it is important to unmask and heal our racism and serve others in need, not for the purpose of converting them but because—and only because—it is the right thing to do.

CULTIVATING NON-SEXUAL INTIMACY WITH OTHERS

People recovering from fundamentalism often report feeling lonely because they have lost their sense of community. Losing one's community under any circumstance can be disorienting and leave one feeling bereft of friends. Fundamentalists have been taught to be suspicious of people who are not born-again Christians. Unbelievers can "lead them astray" or "lead them into temptation." One is only really "safe" with others who have accepted Jesus as their personal savior, and even then, one must remain vigilant and judgmental because another Christian's relationship with God may not be as "pure" as one's own, or conversely, another Christian's relationship with God may look so solid and flawless that one is left with feelings of inferiority and shame regarding their own. In other words, God is always involved in every relationship in terms of how much and how well one lives their Christian life. It is never about relating to another Christian as a human being outside of their relationship with God, but always judging how well the other person is walking with God—and of course, presenting to others how one's own life conforms to the rules of the game. I use the word "game" intentionally because friendships among fundamentalists are almost always, on some level, a game. How well are we doing with Jesus? Do you have more points than I have or vice-versa?

For this reason, making friends with people on the basis of human connection may feel strange or even bewildering outside the rules of the Jesus game. It means seeing the other person as an ordinary human being just as they are and for who they are without Jesus. It also means allowing another person to see your naked human being-ness. For fundamentalists, making new friendships with nonfundamentalists can feel clumsy or pointless. After all, what do we have in common? If we're not playing the Jesus game, what *are* we doing?

In the fundamentalist world, other people are actually objects, and you yourself are an object, according to Marlene Winell. Your "human nature" is inherently evil and must be cleansed by the born-again experience. The apostle John said, "He must increase, and I must decrease"—a phrase often heard among fundamentalists, which Winell states is a process of self-annihilation in order to be the best Christian you can be. In fundamentalism, people make objects of other people for the purpose of conversion or for the purpose of fellowship. Unbelievers are the "lost sheep" who aren't "saved" and have no knowledge of God's plan. There is no point in having empathy with their suffering because they may be experiencing God's punishment, or perhaps they would not be suffering at all if they were born-again. Believers are sacred and safe objects with whom you can have fellowship in order to improve your Jesus game and theirs.

DEVELOPING INTIMACY WITH NATURE

Fundamentalists have been taught to devalue and minimize nature because they believe that in the Book of Genesis, God told humans to "have dominion" over the earth. From my perspective, this command is the first tragedy in the story of separation—the belief that humans are separate from nature, have nothing to learn from it, should dominate and "tame" nature, and that any reverence for nature borders on paganism or witchcraft.

In church, people may sing "For the beauty of the earth, for the glory of the skies," and have no idea what they are singing. The earth is not something to be dominated but is rather a glorious work of art and science that lives in the very cells of our bodies. Almost all of the elements of the earth are found in the human body; therefore, it is impossible to separate ourselves from nature.

I heartily recommend that people recovering from religious trauma or abuse should discover the healing power of spending quality time in nature—not labeling or identifying or quantifying, but simply enjoying the solitude, sensuality, beauty, sounds, and smells of nature. How beautiful it is to approach nature with the innocence of a child. Listen to it, observe it, feel it. Don't just say that it is God's creation and God should be praised because without God, it wouldn't exist. When I chased butterflies in my mother's garden as a child, I didn't say, "Oh, this butterfly was made by God." I simply chased them, marveled at their colors, and felt a magical sense of wonder in my body when butterflies appeared.

Evangelical climate scientist, Katherine Hayhoe, states that, "We humans have been given responsibility for every living thing on this planet, which includes each other. We are called to tend the garden and be good stewards of the gifts that God has given us."[7] And yet few evangelicals or fundamentalist Christians take climate science seriously. In fact, most are skeptical of science at best and actively anti-science at worst.

EXPERIENCING THE JOY OF LIVING

An old Christian Sunday School song says, "I've got the joy, joy, joy, joy down in my heart...." The topic of "joy" is popular in fundamentalist circles because they have so often been seen as rigid, pious, strict, and harsh—in fact, they are, and they *know* they are. Hence, the emphasis on showing the world how happy and joyful they feel. We have only to look at the megachurch extravaganzas with rock bands, light shows, dazzling and fiery sermons, and emotionally gushing altar calls. Being baptized with the Holy Spirit and speaking in tongues is yet another level of temporary ecstasy which gives oxygen to the illusion of joy.

Yet I would argue that very few fundamentalists feel the joy of being alive in a body on planet Earth. There simply is no joy of living without playing the Jesus game. In fact, being disembodied (not fully present in the body), disconnected from nature, disconnected from so-called negative emotions, and disconnected from the humanity of others, is a profoundly joyless existence.

In order to experience and savor the joy of one's humanity and the humanity of others, it is necessary, in my opinion, to move beyond fundamentalist programming and discover pure joy and the full spectrum of human emotion outside of the Jesus game. It may take years to learn how to live without the fundamentalist worldview, and the deconstruction of it and the reconstruction of a new life will be challenging, messy, and humbling, but as Marlene Winell says, if you dare to live, you will find your way. [8]

As you continue to recover from religious trauma, you will discover how not-alive you have been taught to be and how much the fullness of living is awaiting you as an embodied human being in this amazing world. Rather than continually asking, "What is God's will for me?" you might begin to ask instead, "What makes me truly alive?" As the great American author and theologian Howard Thurman wrote:

> Don't ask what the world needs. Ask what makes you come alive, and go do it. Because what the world needs is people who have come alive.[9]

Following is a checklist for determining if a religion, spiritual teaching, or organization is functional and life-affirming.

CONFRONTING CHRISTOFASCISM

YOUR SPIRITUAL PATH IS FUNCTIONAL IF...

- It does not require you to follow the teachings of sacred texts or the rules of a religious or spiritual organization.
- It is not an authoritarian or hierarchical path.
- It does not question scientific facts or findings.
- It supports you in treating illness with traditional medicine or natural medicine but does not assert that one form of treatment is better than another.
- It supports you in seeking mental and emotional health treatment and counseling from people outside the organization.
- It supports you in feeling your feelings and questioning its teachings and encourages you to think for yourself and cultivate discernment.
- It supports you in understanding personal boundaries and maintaining them for your own well-being.
- It does not threaten you with the punishment of eternal damnation or promise you eternal bliss depending on how you follow your path.
- It does not require you to practice your spiritual path in a particular way.
- It does not ask you to follow God's will instead of your intellect and intuition.
- It does not encourage you to consult spiritual guides or teachers before making decisions. You can choose to consult them or not.
- It does not teach that you are inherently sinful, defective, weak, ignorant, or unenlightened.
- It supports you in questioning everything it believes.
- It does not shame you for who you are or for disagreeing with any person or group.

- It does not condemn your sexual orientation or gender identity.
- It does not state or imply that men are superior and women are inferior.
- It does not discriminate against you on the basis of ethnicity or skin color.
- It does not offer rules regarding contraception or abortion.
- It does not require you to educate your children in a particular belief system.
- It does not require you to remain in any relationship with an abusive person.
- It encourages you to become a whole person by educating yourself, appreciating the arts, and engaging in your own creative expressions.
- It deeply respects nature and the environment and does not teach that humans must have dominion over them.
- It does not subscribe to specific political beliefs and does not pressure you to agree with those beliefs.

8. CONFRONTING KU KLUX CHRISTIANITY

I would rather have questions that can't be answered than answers that can't be questioned.
—Richard Feynman[1]

The purpose of separation of church and state is to keep forever from these shores the ceaseless strife that has soaked the soil of Europe in blood for centuries.
—James Madison

Germany was not only the birthplace of modern fascism, but it also gave us the life and legacy of Martin Luther, who believed that God divinely grants power to political leaders. Just as today we look back on Germany in the 1930s and ask why the German people embraced Hitler and the Nazi Party, will we look back from some future date and wonder why millions of white Christians, specifically evangelicals, voted for Donald Trump twice and and supported the neo-fascist policies of the Republican Party? What will be the result of this support?

As Portland journalist, D.L. Mayfield points out in her article, "The Good White Christian Women of Nazi Germany," a song popular in Germany before Hitler pleaded, "Oh God, send us a Führer who will change our misfortune by God's word." Many Germans "loved this song which welcomed Hitler because Germany needed a strong man sent by God to beat the threat of communists." Mayfield notes that good Christian women supported Nazism because it benefited them, and it seemed to reinforce the cultural values that gave meaning and purpose to their lives. They believed God was in control and had blessed their culture and their leader with special greatness —and that outsiders and foreign influence needed to be subjugated or eradicated in order for Germans to protect themselves.[2]

As mentioned above, since the election of Donald Trump in 2016, more people than I recall have personally asked me how it is that evangelical Christians could not only vote for him, but continue to support him throughout his Presidency, then vote for him again in 2020.

I continue to answer with three simple realities: *Fear of people of color, fear of legal abortion,* and *fear of marriage equality.* In fact, this is what evangelical Christianity in America has become—a fear-fueled crusade of racism, sexism, and homophobia that has absolutely nothing to do with the teachings of Jesus in the New Testament. If this is true, then a significant portion of evangelicals are now operating out of hysteria rather than analytical thought and rational behavior. Notable exceptions are climate scientist Katherine Hayhoe, Bible teacher Beth Moore (who has left the Southern Baptist Church), and Russell Moore (no relation to Beth), a prominent Southern Baptist leader, who are willing to pay the price of confronting the bigoted aspects of their religion.

FUNDAMENTALISM FUELS NONSENSICAL THINKING

As we have seen, American fundamentalism erupted out of an irrational fear of cultural change in the late nineteenth century. Protestantism itself, although a noble rebellion against the authoritarianism of the Roman Catholic Church, rapidly became spiritually, emotionally, and politically authoritarian. Luther and Calvin were rigorously patriarchal and used their essentially remarkable intellects to construct theologies that continue to damage and degrade humanity to this day. But the Christian story itself, which commenced in the first century, was marinated in authoritarian thinking.

When reading the Synoptic Gospels of Matthew, Mark, and Luke, we see a Jesus who did not consider himself separate from the world. He lived and moved *in* the world with compassion, inclusivity, justice, and courage. The divergent Gospel of John, written decades after the Synoptic Gospels, depicts a more separatist Jesus (in the world but not of it), and a Jesus who insists that he and he alone is "the way." In the Synoptic Gospels, Jesus did command his apostles to spread the good news throughout the world, but as I have emphasized, the good news was that all people are unconditionally accepted and loved by God. Very quickly, the good news became the bad news of "ye must be born again....or else."

Progressive Franciscan priest, Richard Rohr, writes in his 2021 book, *The Universal Christ*, that, "We worshipped Jesus instead of following him on the same path. We made Jesus into a mere religion instead of a journey toward union with God and everything else. This shift made us into a religion of belonging and believing instead of a religion of transformation."[3]

For the most part, Jews rejected the Christian message, and the apostles then spread it throughout the Roman Empire to people whom Christians called pagan because they worshipped many deities. In that milieu, conversion was actually unknown because polytheism was perfectly acceptable. However, the Christian gospel very quickly became dogmatically exclusive. As historian Bart Ehrman points out:

> And so Christians believed that their religion was the only right religion and that people had to practice their religion, or else they would go to hell. Moreover, Christians maintained that they were to follow Jesus' teachings of love. You were to love your neighbor as yourself. Well, if your neighbor's going to go to hell by not believing what you believe and you love this person, then you need to make them see the error of their ways and convert them to your faith. And so that's what Christians were doing from the very beginning, trying to convert others so that they could join the church and avoid the terrors of hell.
>
> …they thought they had the right understanding of salvation, but they were very insistent that they alone were right. People who are convinced that they have a corner on the truth naturally try to convince other people to agree with them. And so Christians had a kind of vested interest in promoting their own point of view because they thought they were right, and if more people agreed that they're right then that convinces them that they really are right. And so there certainly were some ulterior motives in the Christian mission.[4]

Critical thinking is the ability to think clearly and rationally about what to do or what to believe. It includes the ability to engage in reflective and independent thinking.[5] When one is committed to an authoritarian perspective, it is virtually impossible to think critically. Conversely, here is what critical thinkers do:

- Understand the logical connections between ideas
- Identify, construct, and evaluate arguments

- Detect inconsistencies and common mistakes in reasoning
- Solve problems systematically
- Identify the relevance and importance of ideas
- Reflect on the justification of one's own beliefs and values

CONFRONTING ANCESTRAL ROOTS OF RACISM

Most white people in the United States are not intentionally racist; however, we do not become racist consciously. Racism is ingrained in us throughout our lives through white privilege. According to Wikipedia, "White privilege is the societal privilege that benefits white people over non-white people in some societies, particularly if they are otherwise under the same social, political, or economic circumstances."[6] If we are aware of our ancestry at all, we rarely consider whether or not our ancestors oppressed people of color. Even if one was born in the North and had Abolitionist ancestors, earlier generations of our relatives were influenced by or participated in white supremacy. As noted above, Christian fundamentalism was founded by white males, many of them veterans or descendants of veterans of the Civil War.

Sarah Stankorb, in her online article, "White Evangelical Racism Has Always Been a Political Power Grab," interviews Anthea Butler about her latest book, *White Evangelical Racism.* She writes that "racism is original to the fabric of evangelicalism." Butler draws lines from Biblical references used in defense of slavery, through Reconstruction, when Black men were framed as a sexual menace against virtuous white women, to evangelical believers and churches engaged in lynching. Butler demonstrates how political organizing by the Christian Right in the 1970s (prior to *Roe v. Wade*) was actually a first response to desegregation and the end of interracial marriage bans. That power coalesced and became institutionalized in such a way that evangelicalism was no longer exactly a religious designation, but a political one.[7]

This is not to say that there are no people of color in evangelical churches. Indeed there are, but almost without exception, they are committed to the evangelical worldview. In this way, Christians of color have become "neutered" because their focus is not on racial justice, ending poverty, or confronting the social justice issues that permeate communities of color. Rather, their mission, like that of their fellow white parishioners, is evangelism and fellowshipping with other born-again Christians. As Butler emphasizes, it is whites who have the power in evangelical circles.

One of many examples of this reality is the evangelical African American minister Jesse Lee Peterson, who recently declared in an interview with a white, female, right-wing Christian interviewer, that "we must remember white history, because if it wasn't for that, there would be no America." He also bashed LGBTQ Pride month and emphasized that, "...not one Christian should be celebrating gay pride. They should be praying that these people repent and overcome their fallen state and return to the father. God is not pleased that his children are allowing this." Furthermore, Peterson stated that he doesn't believe the story of the Tulsa Race Massacre and added that, "Black people are not telling the truth."[8]

What also must be noted is the increase of Latino evangelicals in the United States and in Latin American countries. The majority are politically conservative, and many supported the election of Donald Trump in 2016 and 2020. Writing in the inclusive Christian magazine *Sojourner*, Aaron Sanchez stated in 2019 that "the politics and experiences of Latino evangelicals place them and their national leaders in a difficult position. The rhetoric and policies of the Trump administration directly threatens Latino evangelicals, who are overwhelmingly young, poor, immigrants. The blanket statements from Trump that portray brown bodies as inherently criminal and an invading force, runs counter to the ways that large swaths of them understand themselves as humans and Christians. For many Latino evangelicals, their faith is the very way they challenge their dehumanization. Their belief that they are beloved children of God challenges their marginalization and demonization. However, key leaders...support Trump and increasingly support authoritarian leaders in Latin America with evangelical ties. They believe that these politicians are doing God's work, even while they attack the most vulnerable of God's people."[9]

AMERICAN THEOCRACY

Throughout the four years of the Trump Administration we witnessed a regime that displayed staggering incompetence in governing, and that could never hide its abject contempt for government itself. Never before in American history had we seen the numbers of people appointed to official positions in the Administration who so blatantly displayed such lack of qualifications and experience in relation their job descriptions. Early on, it was painfully obvious that the Trump Administration was not only incompetent, it actually hated government. In the infamous words of Presidential Advisor Steve Bannon, the overriding goal of the administration was to "deconstruct the administrative state." Bannon is a neo-fascist and a white supremacist, and his ideal administration would not be a democratic republic, but an autocratic dictatorship. And yet the Trump Administration was replete with born-again Christians like Mike Pompeo, Secretary of State; Betsy DeVos, Secretary of Education; Mike Pence, Vice-President; Ben Carson, Secretary of Housing and Urban Development; and Robert Redfield, Director of the Center for Disease Control. Their agenda varied only slightly from Bannon's in that they too wanted to deconstruct government as we have known it, but replace it with a theocracy, or government by God.

Earlier, I referred to author Kevin Phillips. During the George W. Bush Administration, he wrote *American Theocracy*, in which he warned readers of rule by "divine authority," which he believed was solidifying in the policies of oil politics, fundamentalist Christianity, and the financialization of the American economy. Yet I doubt that Phillips could have imagined what the Trump Administration would be laying out and implementing only ten years after he wrote his book.

But why would fundamentalists want a government by God in the end times when they were living day by day for the Rapture? Quite simply, from their perspective, a theocracy would hasten the Rapture and the fulfillment of the apocalyptic prophecies that their every thought, word, and deed hung on. Moreover, they would want to live in a world, whatever the duration of that world, where they mingled with whites only, where abortion was illegal, and where the LGBTQ community lived in constant fear of punishment.

Radical right-wing pastor Greg Locke in 2020 declared that "...there is no reason the church of the living God and the kingdom of Jesus Christ should not rule this nation. Those that truly follow Jesus Christ [should] take it by force!"[10] We don't know exactly what the theocracy of Locke's dreams would look like, but "The Handmaid's Tale"[11] might give us a clue.

In fact, it may be that many fundamentalist Christians are consciously or unconsciously becoming impatient with the Rapture. They have waited so long for it that part of their audacious insistence regarding theocracy may stem from "rapture anticipation fatigue." Curiously, a recent movement, the New Apostolic Reformation (NAR), is advocating theocracy as the ideal replacement for democracy. The NAR is a title originally used by C. Peter Wagner to describe a movement within Pentecostal and charismatic churches which advocates theocratic control in seven areas identified specifically: religion, family, education, government, media, arts and entertainment, and business. [12]

In "The New Apostolic Reformation and the Theology of Prosperity: The 'Kingdom of God' as a Hermeneutical Key," Martin Ocana cites one example:

> Democracy, in all of its expressions, will always be a barrier to the kingdom of the apostles. Some of these even come to say in the Church that "a good dictatorship is better—theirs—than a bad democracy." It can legitimately be said that the final project of the NAR is to impose their idea of "theocracy" onto society as a whole, if they ever get the opportunity to reign amongst it. However, it would be better if they would state clearly and without ambiguities that what they propose to achieve is an "apostolic world government" (and not precisely *the Kingdom of God*). Their position has generated a series of reactions that are justified from every point of view. [13]

Ocana summarizes the NAR by adding that, "... by what we have seen, the NAR is a contemporary religious movement with great political ambitions. To achieve their political purpose it does not hesitate to go to the metaphor...of the 'Kingdom of God,' which occupies an important place in their arguments. But the Kingdom of God—in the perspective of the NAR—has a location and an earthly content. *The goal of the NAR is the construction of the Kingdom of God on earth. They believe that such an undertaking is possible.* And the apostles, and the movement itself, have a preponderant role in it." [14]

In other words, democracy stands in the way of fundamentalist and charismatic notions of theocracy and must be sacrificed so that the Kingdom of God can be established. As of the first half of 2021, one political party in the United States no longer believes in democracy. In fact, it is at war with the American experiment, and that party is overwhelmingly supported by people who identify as evangelicals. Many Americans are unable to fathom the realities of this political moment. "The United States couldn't possibly morph into a fascist dictatorship," they say. "The January 6, 2021 insurrection was a one-time event. If we just move on, it won't happen again."

It is not an exaggeration to declare that the Republican Party has declared war on democracy, nor is it a stretch to assume that the overthrow of the American republic, the direct intent of January 6, is now the protracted agenda of those involved in creating and carrying out the insurrection. What is the "traveling circus" of 2020 election audits we have seen in states like Arizona and heading for a host of other states, if not insurrection? What is the introduction of voter suppression laws in at least 47 states if not a slow-moving insurgency movement designed to eliminate the U.S. Constitution?

You may argue that you are not political and do not wish to become involved in the controversies of one or the other political party. While I appreciate this perspective, the blinding reality is that if you have been actively involved with Christian fundamentalism, you are *already* politically involved and have been involved in a Christofascist jihad that is willing to sacrifice democracy in order to establish what it believes is God's kingdom on earth. I do not mean that you personally are condoning Christofascism, but American fundamentalism, even before the birth of the Religious Right or the Trump Presidency, has been a proselytizing, colonizing jihad, committed to using any means necessary to accomplish its mission. A *Rolling Stone* article written a few weeks after the January 6 insurrection clarifies in disgusting detail "How the Christian Right Helped Foment Insurrection."[15] One fundamentalist who stormed the Capitol said, "God told me to let the church roar."[16]

Conversely, for some people, actively working to weaken the

influence of Christian fundamentalism and its assaults on democracy can be healing and restorative.

THE GHOST OF JOHN SCOPES

When individuals cannot think critically, and when they have been conditioned for decades to believe that science is the enemy, it is not surprising to see widespread climate change denial among evangelicals. For many, climate science is simply a hoax, but for those incessantly trolling for "signs and wonders" of the Rapture, dramatic climate events and natural disasters are indicative of the end times. My father, a rabid Pentecostal, believed that climate change was evidence of God's judgment on humans for their sinful ways and proof that the Rapture was imminent.

Evangelical climate scientist, Katherine Hayhoe[17] is a notable and noble exception to the spectrum of evangelicals who are climate change deniers. According to Hayhoe, the fact remains that from the 1970s through the 1990s, American liberals and conservatives trusted science, and scientists, at roughly equal levels, but since the 1990s, while liberals' trust in science has gone up, conservatives' trust has gone down. This disparity has increased in recent years as Republicans have moved more to the political right in their beliefs, coinciding with an anti-science sentiment, and leading to condemnations of science and higher education among some Republicans.[18]

The anti-vaccine movement, climate change denial, protests against stem cell research, and other movements such as these are rooted in the spread of disinformation and a distrust of science. Many evangelical children are homeschooled, where they are taught intelligent design (the notion that life on Earth could not have developed solely through scientifically established processes of evolution but instead required the direct intervention of an "intelligent designer") and a companion myth, "young-earth creationism," instead of evolution. Young-earth creationism holds that the Earth and its lifeforms were created in their present forms by supernatural acts of a deity between approximately 6,000 and 10,000 years ago. Additionally, homeschooled evangelical children are often warned that stem cell research, vaccines, and other areas of research in the biological sciences are examples of humans trying to be like God.

Throughout the Coronavirus pandemic, we have witnessed countless stories of evangelicals who scoffed at the virus as a hoax or as a plot to prevent Christians from gathering in groups or as an ailment as harmless as the flu that has been exaggerated by the liberal left. At this writing, 45% of evangelicals say they will not be vaccinated, and the highest percentage of those are white males.[19] Some evangelicals declare that receiving the vaccine is the equivalent of receiving "the mark of the Beast"—the prophecy in the Book of Revelation that in the end times, people will be required to receive the physical labeling of the anti-Christ in order to be able to buy food and survive.

A CULTURE OF CARING IS "SOCIALISM"

Overwhelmingly, evangelicals and Ronald Reagan's trickle-down austerity are joined at the hip as if the teachings of Jesus never existed. For poor and working class evangelicals, the notion of economic equality is totalitarianism, and the desire for racial justice will invariably result in the extermination of the white race. Caring for one's own family and fellow-believers is acceptable, but unbelievers, particularly if they are people of color, have brought their misery upon themselves and do not deserve mercy. For Congressional Republicans schooled in Ayn Rand, "the virtue of selfishness" is the new Golden Rule. Evangelicals with hollowed-out hearts, so reminiscent of the "good Christian women of Nazi Germany," preen themselves with their piety and capitulate to every policy that is in their self-interest, with compassion for no one, devoid of any visceral appreciation of democracy or any willingness to fight for it. And we wonder why "good Christians" vacuously prayed for "a new Führer" in the 1930s and were more than willing in 2016 and 2020 to surrender to Trump's establishment of "the Nation of MAGA-stan"? The Sermon on the Mount be damned.

Former President Lyndon Johnson said it best: "I'll tell you what's at the bottom of it. If you can convince the lowest white man he's better than the best colored man, he won't notice you're picking his pocket. Hell, give him somebody to look down on, and he'll empty his pockets for you."[20]

RELIGIOUS NATIONALISM AND CONSPIRACY

During the Presidency of Donald Trump, conspiracy theory groups have attracted numerous evangelicals. As noted above, right-wing evangelicals, steeped in their doctrines, have fewer critical thinking skills and are not particularly concerned with fact-checking or research integrity.

"I'm actually not surprised that evangelicals are more likely to believe those kinds of things," said Samuel Perry, a professor of sociology at the University of Oklahoma. "Evangelicals are not socially isolated, but they are informationally isolated."[21]

Kaleigh Rogers in her article, "Why QAnon Has Attracted So Many White Evangelicals," quotes Perry, who adds that:

> The narrative of QAnon, of Donald Trump as this lone warrior who nobody understands and nobody believes but who is fighting the good fight, I think they identify with that. They feel themselves misunderstood and victimized and that they are fighting the good fight that nobody recognizes.

But, says Rogers, perhaps the biggest connection between the world of QAnon and the world of evangelical Christians is one that's much harder to quantify and capture, but it seems obvious when talking to someone from either group. The QAnon movement has suffered multiple failed prophecies, predictions about events that never came to pass. To continue holding onto beliefs in spite of those disappointments, followers need something many evangelicals have in spades: faith.[22]

Conspiracy theories can be very attractive for fundamentalist Christians. The mindset of "us and them" and the centuries-old belief that Christians always have been and always will be persecuted makes them vulnerable to anticipating persecution and seeing it where it does not exist.

Think about it: Isn't Christian fundamentalism one enormous conspiracy theory in itself?

"The world doesn't understand us; the world is deceived by the devil and does his work by persecuting us." In fact, being persecuted is a badge of honor in this worldview because one can follow in the footsteps of Jesus, the apostles, and a host of early-Church martyrs and feel uniquely special in a particularly toxic manner.

CONFRONTING CHRISTO-FASCISM IN THE CULTURE

In Chapter Seven, I offered numerous suggestions for individuals seeking to heal the evangelical wound and recover from the trauma and pain they have experienced as followers of the evangelical/fundamentalist Christian path. While an individual's recovery may be challenging, if not agonizing at times, it is certainly not as daunting as the task of pulling an entire culture back from the brink of authoritarianism.

Certainly, no individual is capable of doing so. Creating a bulwark against fascism in American culture requires groups of individuals committed to political action and social justice. This may be especially challenging for those recovering from Christian fundamentalism. It is a formidable task for any American, but those indoctrinated with religious conspiracy theories may find it a particularly onerous task. On the other hand, I have known many former fundamentalists who are deeply engaged in confronting the rising tide of fascism *because* they lived through and survived religious mind manipulation.

If you are newly recovering from fundamentalism, you may not be inclined to engage in political discussion or action, and that is absolutely fine. Your first obligation is to your own healing. However, if you feel up to the task, before you act, you must understand the full implications of any form of authoritarianism that claims divine authority.

I grew up in the 1950s during the Red Scare of the McCarthy era. Joseph McCarthy, a paranoid and opportunist Senator from Wisconsin, embarked on a crusade to rid the United States of communism and anyone who embraced communism. In the process, he destroyed many lives and reputations. His right-hand man was an attorney named Roy Cohn, who later became the principal mentor of Donald Trump. While the authoritarianism of Russia was dark and deadly on many levels, the authoritarianism of McCarthy and his far-right conservative cohorts was equally destructive.

History is replete with religious leaders who ordered mass killings and the genocide of entire populations because they would not convert to Christianity. Our own American continent could not have been fully developed without the genocide of millions of Native Americans—a far larger number of souls than were killed in the Jewish holocaust of the Second World War.

Donald Trump was and is a neo-fascist. Had he been re-elected we would have experienced a full-on fascist autocracy in the United States during his second term and certainly in the subsequent terms that he was determined to have. Should he be re-elected, he will become an incontestable dictator. He and his supporters did everything in their power to nullify the election of President Biden, including launch an insurrection at the United States Capitol on January 6, 2021 with the intention of overturning the 2020 election and capturing and killing then Vice-President, Mike Pence, a born-again Christian, and House Speaker, Nancy Pelosi. Many Americans, especially fundamentalist Christians who supported Trump, do not realize how close the nation came to a violent revolution on January 6. While it was a brutal event in which five people died, it was not an overthrow of democracy, but that was the direct intent of the insurrectionists.

What is more, the people who participated in the insurrection and the politicians who supported—even helped them—that day, have not gone away. In fact, many of those politicians are members of the Republican Party. They consider Donald Trump the legitimate President of the United States because they insist, contrary to historical fact, that the 2020 election was stolen from him. The insurrectionists and the politicians who support them have been mindlessly influenced by conspiracy theories that embrace authoritarianism, white supremacy, the subjugation of women and the LGBTQ community, a return of the Civil War Confederacy, and for some, a long-awaited American theocracy.

As a result of the Trump Presidency and the January 6 insurrection, the United States sits at an inflection point between democracy and authoritarianism as one political party overwhelmingly surrenders to fascist ideology, courted and coddled by the Religious Right. We do not know if the Biden Presidency can transcend the onslaughts of voter suppression, brutal economic austerity, white supremacy, and weekly mass shootings facilitated by Republican intransigence around gun laws. What we do know is that people of conscience cannot be neutral in the battle for the soul of democracy. Virulent political fascism is being facilitated and financed by the Religious Right, and as author and Presbyterian minister Chris Hedges writes, "The fascist movement in America will not display itself with swastikas and brown shirts, but will instead wrap itself around the Christian cross and American flag."[23]

THE WORSENING CRISIS OF AUTHORITARIANISM

If we observe other countries that have declined from open or democratic societies to becoming authoritarian regimes, we notice that in most cases, the decline was gradual. While there are many instances of sudden upheaval and abrupt change, even these had their roots in subtle and deepening cracks in the foundations of those governments. For example, Viktor Orban came to power in Hungary in 2010 and strengthened a fascist movement that was already growing in popularity. Other countries where we have seen the rise of authoritarianism in recent times are Brazil, the Philippines, Belarus, Iran, and Saudi Arabia.

Both Professors Timothy Snyder and Jason Stanley, mentioned earlier in this book, have written extensively about fascism and the stages of its unfolding in the modern world. According to them and others who have studied the rise of authoritarian governments, the United States is at a critical juncture.

A NEW DEFINITION OF PATRIOTISM

Perhaps you were raised in a fundamentalist Christian family where you learned that being a good American was being a born-again Christian. You may have been taught that "freedom" is the freedom to worship God in the way you choose, go to the church of your choice, preach the gospel, or pray in school. Many Christians today define freedom as the "right" not to wear a mask or the right to own a gun. And whether or not you were homeschooled or attended public school, most Americans with a high school education do not have a full understanding of our Constitution and what the founders of our country intended—and did not intend—in creating a democratic republic.

In my journey of moving beyond fundamentalism, I found that studying American history in depth removed many misconceptions I had about "freedom," "democracy," and "God and country." The study of history was an enormous boon to my abandoning the fundamentalist worldview, and I highly recommend studying history. Also, studying the roots of racism in our country will help you begin to heal the racism with which all white people in America are tragically tainted.

When we explore American history, we realize that our founders were far from perfect. They were overwhelmingly privileged white slave owners. Most of them were atheists or agnostics. Yet in the late eighteenth century, they cobbled together a form of government that has lasted two and a half centuries.

Now in 2021 we are dangerously at risk of losing the imperfect democracy that the founders created. We are at risk not only because of a groundswell of fascist ideology that led to the January 6 insurrection, but because climate chaos and deep chasms of political division may actually lead to the collapse of systems and ultimately, Western civilization itself.

The Capitol insurrection of January 6, 2021 was not an isolated event. When we listen carefully to members of the Republican Party, it is obvious that most do not believe that Donald Trump lost the 2020 election, but that it was stolen from him. They are currently attacking voting rights in at least half of the states in the country, and what is even more chilling than the attack on voting rights is the ultimate goal of eliminating voting itself. Who needs elections when a permanently-installed leader—who will maintain white supremacy, make all abortion in the United States illegal, and suppress and even eliminate members of the LGBTQ community in the name of God—holds such absolute power that the legislative and judicial systems exist only to do his bidding?

If we truly understand and value the fragile democracy we still have, we must be engaged in actions that protect and preserve it.

TAKING A STAND FOR HUMAN DIGNITY

Human dignity—two words rarely used by divinity-dazzled fundamentalists—is the touchstone of being human. Jesus and many of the world's great wisdom teachers embodied and lived it. While we could debate its meaning *ad infinitum*, we all know instinctively what it means, because when our human dignity is violated, we feel it in every fiber of our being.

Taking a stand for human dignity means:

- Defending the right of people to breathe clean air, eat safe and nourishing food, and drink clean water.
- Defending the right of people to have shelter and a safe place to live
- Defending the right of people to have gainful employment
- Defending the right of people of color to have the rights guaranteed to them by the Constitution
- Defending the right of all people of voting age to register to vote, to be able to vote without racial discrimination or fear of intimidation, and to have their votes counted fairly
- Defending the right of people to protest peacefully
- Defending the right of women to control their own bodies
- Defending the right of members of the LGBTQ

community to have the same rights as non-members of their community

- Defending the rights of animals to be treated with kindness and care
- Defending the environment and demanding that it be treated with care and respect

Many countries around the world are taking a stand for the rights of the Earth. Some have declared that the Earth is a living being, just as humans are.

In order to confront Christofascism in American culture, we must join organizations, contribute money and time to groups supporting human dignity, peacefully protest, and take our stand in the ways that feel important to us to promote the life and well-being of all living beings. *We do none of this in order to proselytize anyone but because it is the right thing to do.*

We must nominate and vote for candidates that serve human dignity and the natural environment, *and* we must speak out against those who do not. Engagement in social media is vital, as is organizing on behalf of pro-democracy candidates at every level of government. If we are members of churches or religious groups that support fascist principles, (see Chapter 1), we must speak out against authoritarian ideology.

AN URGENT NEED FOR EXEMPLARS

At this watershed moment in the history of the American experiment and democracies everywhere, we desperately need men and women from all spiritual paths who are willing to resist the seductions and the shackles of autocracy. In the throes of the Nazi regime in Germany, Lutheran pastor Dietrich Bonhoeffer wrote that, "Silence in the face of evil is evil itself: God will not hold us guiltless. Not to speak is to speak. Not to act is to act."[24]

Following a visit to England just two days before Hitler's birthday, Bonhoeffer returned to Germany. He, like many German Christians, was repulsed by the German Reich Church or German Evangelical Church, which was antisemitic and racist, adopting as its national symbol a cross with a swastika in the center. The Reich Church ultimately ended up being a confederation of those German Protestant churches that espoused a single doctrine named Positive Christianity, which was compatible with Nazism. Although it aimed to eventually become a unified Protestant state church for all of Nazi Germany, this attempt utterly failed as the German Evangelical Church fractured into various groups that bore an unclear legal status in relation to each other.[25]

Bonhoeffer was famous for his book *The Cost of Discipleship*, but apart from his theological writings, he was known for his staunch resistance to the Nazi dictatorship, including vocal opposition to Hitler's genocidal persecution of the Jews. He was arrested in April 1943 by the Gestapo and imprisoned at Tegel prison for one and a half years. Later, he was transferred to Flossenbürg concentration camp. After being accused of association with the 20 July plot to assassinate Adolf Hitler, he was quickly tried along with other accused plotters, including former members of the *Abwehr* (the German Military Intelligence Office), and then hanged on 9 April 1945, just as the Nazi regime was collapsing.[26]

Nineteenth-century abolitionists in the United States struggled to make Christianity a religion of freedom rather than slavery. William Lloyd Garrison, not a Christian but a deist, founded the abolitionist newspaper *The Liberator*, whose masthead had an image of Jesus looking down on a slave with compassion. Angela and Sarah Grimke were Christian women who grew up in the South and decided that slavery was sinful. Harriett Beecher Stowe, author of *Uncle Tom's Cabin*, grew up in a religious family. Three of her brothers became pro-abolitionist ministers.

Dorothy Day was a journalist turned social activist who became known for her social justice campaigns in defense of the poor. Alongside Peter Maurin, she founded the Catholic Worker Movement in 1933, espousing nonviolence and hospitality for the impoverished and downtrodden.

Simone Weil was a French philosopher who, early in her life, was animated by a great compassion for the exploited. She was first a socialist, then an anarchist. In 1930s, she converted to the "love of Christ." During her experience, she explains that she suddenly felt that Christianity was the religion of the slaves, and that she, like other slaves, could not resist adhering to it. She is considered a "Christian mystic" and an "anarchist Christian."

In the twenty-first century, Christian activists such as Reverend Al Sharpton, Bishop William Barber, and U.S. Senator Reverend Raphael Warnock are calling out religious authoritarianism and championing social justice within the framework of our constitutional, democratic republic.

More recently, Reverend Russell Moore has become a renegade evangelical who has departed from the Southern Baptist Convention (SBC), the largest Baptist denomination in the United States. According to the *Atlantic*, "His departure was not primarily prompted, as many people had assumed, by his role as an outspoken critic of Donald Trump, although that had clearly upset powerful members within the politically and theologically conservative denomination. Instead, the letter suggests, the breach was caused by the stands he had taken against sexual abuse within the SBC and on racial reconciliation, which had infuriated the executive committee."[27]

Beth Moore, not related to Reverend Russell Moore, also left the SBC, stating, "Nonetheless, something has gone awry; the revelations contained in Russell Moore's letter were only the latest links in a disturbingly long chain of offenses." She also cited the "staggering" disorientation of seeing denominational leaders support Trump and denounced the "demonic stronghold" of white supremacy and "the sexism and misogyny that is rampant in segments of the SBC."[28]

Sadly, most people of faith worldwide are either oblivious to the looming demise of democracy or are in denial of it. All who claim to practice the teachings of Jesus must recognize Christofascism for what it is and expose those who embrace and enable it.

SEEKING UNITY WITH EVANGELICALS

Yet isn't part of the good news that Jesus gave us through his teachings the command to love everyone and seek to heal any divisions we have with them? Absolutely. Jesus was unequivocally clear about this. So what does living the teachings of Jesus in 2021 look like in relation to misguided fundamentalists who support Donald Trump and who are at war with democracy because they believe they are actually attempting to establish God's kingdom on earth?

If you are a recovering fundamentalist who no longer identifies with your former religion, you probably already know that attempting to reason with a devout fundamentalist is virtually impossible. They do not understand or care to understand critical thinking. They are obsessed with defending their faith. Scientific research matters little to them, if at all. They approach any discussion with laser fixation on their number one mission in life: To save souls and live a model Christian life as they understand that notion, based on a literal interpretation of the Bible. For them, *conversation* is synonymous with *conversion*. Having an open, honest, rational conversation in which both parties respect the opinions of the other and still disagree is virtually impossible. It was the American comedian, the late Dick Gregory, who said, "Ask yourself, 'is this person mentally mature enough to grasp the concept of different perspective?' If not, there is no point to argue."[29]

Therefore, I have long since abandoned the ideal of being able to dialog with fundamentalists. What I find much more useful and less frustrating for myself is to ask them questions about what they believe and simply listen to their answers. I said "less frustrating" because hearing a fundamentalist proclaim their belief system is highly frustrating for me, but not as odious as being a target of their evangelism. By listening actively to the answers to your questions, bearing in mind what you have read in Chapter 3 of this book, you will at least be engaging with another human being in authentic communication, but bear in mind that listening is probably the best you can hope for in this regard. At the same time, it is important to maintain strong boundaries and ward off any attempts to convert you. Listening to what matters to your fundamentalist conversation partner will evoke all kinds of emotions in you, and hopefully, compassion will be one of them. By listening, you are likely to hear the ocean of fear in which they swim, their seemingly bottomless pit of shame, and their stark disconnection from reality.

In addition, I have found that it is important in conversations with fundamentalist Christians to declare alliance with Jesus and his teachings. They are likely to quickly move from hearing your alliance with Jesus to pointing out that his teachings alone do not include the full scope of what they consider "the good news." To be a faithful born-again Christian, they argue, one must include the teachings of Paul and the early Christian theologians. Nevertheless, bringing the focus back to Jesus and his teachings is basic.

Author, speaker, and theological scholar Benjamin Corey writes that "the most interesting biblical hermeneutic [interpretation] is the one that sees Paul's statements on women as permanent injunctions for all time, but sees Jesus' command to love enemies as being so strangely full of nuance that it never seems to apply."[30]

It is also possible to engage in reflective listening with your conversation partner. This means that you reflect back to them what you are hearing about their experience. For example, fundamentalist Christians love to give their "testimony," which means telling the story of their born-again experience. You can actually ask them to tell you the story and then reflect back to them what you hear, such as: "It sounds like you were really desperate when you became a Christian," or "It sounds like your conversion has really given meaning to your life." Reflective listening is a useful way to take the focus off of yourself and keep it on them.

EVANGELICAL IDENTITY IS ABSOLUTELY POLITICAL

In a recent podcast with the *Atlantic Magazine* entitled, "'Evangelical' is Not a Religious Identity, It's a Political One," an interviewer is speaking with fundamentalist icon and American political consultant and lobbyist Ralph Reed. In the podcast, Reed not only shares his conversion experience but gives an in-depth account of his dogged commitment to conservative politics. Reed verbalizes, either explicitly or implicitly, his obsession with the three cultural realities that he and his cohorts simply cannot bear. Perhaps you've already guessed them based on my repeated reminders above: racial equality, abortion, and marriage equality. [31]

Throughout this book I have repeatedly emphasized that Christian fundamentalism in the United States originally erupted as a panicked reaction to cultural changes with which fundamentalists could not abide. It has endured and flourished for more than a century precisely because it offers its followers a way of coping with the culturally unthinkable by providing a psychological escape and the heroic challenge of saving the world from itself. In the process, the movement has become addicted to power and profit. Megachurches have replaced tent meetings, and Ralph Reed has become the R.G. LeTourneau of the twenty-first century. When fundamentalism was birthed, its leaders could only dream of conversing with their Congressman. Today, The Family offers effortless access to Congress and, during the Trump Administration, to Cabinet members and the West Wing itself.

We must never forget that members of the Religious Right unashamedly call themselves Dominionists. The mission of a theocracy is to dominate—and to profit from its dominion. Nor is it only individual megachurches that have big bucks to play with. The *Open Democracy* website in 2020 exposed "the $280 million 'dark money' global empire of the U.S. Christian right." Since 2008, U.S. Christian right groups, many of them linked to the Trump administration and notorious for fighting LGBT and women's reproductive rights, have spent more than $280 million of 'dark money' outside the US. These include the Billy Graham Evangelistic Association, Intervarsity Christian Fellowship, the Federalist Society, Focus on the Family, Human Life International, and the Center for American Law and Justice (ACLJ). Spending by these groups is not exclusively American. Open Democracy reported in 2020 that:

> The ACLJ organization [is] headed by Trump's personal lawyer Jay Sekulow who, along with Rudy Giuliani, coordinated any legal challenges brought by Trump to the result of the US election on 3 November.
>
> Another half-dozen ACLJ lawyers were also part of Trump's defense team in impeachment proceedings earlier this year.
>
> The ACLJ's European branch (the ECLJ) has intervened in two cases to defend Italy's position against gay marriage. It has also intervened in at least seven cases involving Poland, including at the European Court of Human Rights, to defend

that country's conservative policies, including opposition to divorce and abortion.

Poland's constitutional court voted to restrict access to abortion in cases of fatal fetal anomalies. Sekulow's group submitted arguments in favor of the new restrictions.

A second US conservative legal group involved in such cases is Alliance Defending Freedom (ADF). Based in a small town in Arizona, it is also closely linked to the Trump Administration through former staffers and frequent meetings.

ADF went to the US Supreme Court last year to defend nonprofit donor secrecy. The case is still ongoing. Its few known funders include the family foundations of Trump's [former] education secretary Betsy DeVos, also a major Republican party donor.[32]

African American philosophy professor George Yancy wrote, "...my Bible has been taken captive by a fascistic movement masquerading as apocalyptic Christianity. All around this country, we see truth and justice covered with chains, enslaved by selfishness and the lust for power and empire. These are indeed a people who hear and do not understand, see and do not perceive."[33]

According to the Religious News Service, 27 percent of white evangelicals are aligned with QAnon and believe most of its conspiracy theories.[34] To her credit, Jerusha Dufford, granddaughter of Billy Graham, has spoken out against Donald Trump[35] and evangelicals who align with his policies, as have Elizabeth Neumann, and former Southern Baptists Beth Moore and Russell Moore. Nevertheless, while these prominent evangelicals have taken a stand against Christofascist tendencies among their peers, it is not likely that their voices alone can deter the evangelical betrayal of democracy in the long term— certainly not when an overwhelming majority of legislators in the United States Congress are subservient to Donald Trump and the QAnon cult.

THE WHITE EVANGELICAL FASCIST JIHAD

In a recent *UK Independent* article, "QAnon has merged with white Christian evangelicals, experts say—and the results could be lethal," a prominent American researcher of extremism and disinformation, former Congressman Denver Riggleman, states that the connections between QAnon and white evangelical Christianity have "metastasized" into something else that is both "messianic" and "apocalyptic." Riggleman, who was defeated by a far-right primary challenger after officiating at a same-sex wedding and is now chief strategist with the Network Contagion Research Institute, says that the far-right has "... almost become a conspiracy industry that is evangelical." Riggleman said there are parallels between the radicalization process that is being driven by QAnon in the evangelical community and the Islamic radicalism that the US has been trying to combat since 2001: "There certainly is radical Islam, but there's now radicalism on certain evangelical sides, and I think people have been afraid to call it for what it is."[36]

A half-century ago, few fundamentalists could have imagined the political influence they hold today, let alone being a pivotal force in the election of an American President and becoming the backbone of his political base. This book began with an exploration of both fascism and Christian fundamentalism with the intention of highlighting the authoritarian underpinnings of both and the reality that they quite naturally travel together and need each other. As the slow-moving *coup d'etat* launched on January 6, 2021 continues to unfold, we are likely to see further and deeper enmeshment of the two as white supremacy, pro-life, and anti-LGBTQ sentiments render fascism and fundamentalism almost indistinguishable from each other in the political arena.

The long-term causes of the rise of fascism in the United States are numerous, and the role played by evangelical Christianity is only one aspect of the nation's descent into authoritarianism. Yet anyone who is capable of thinking critically and discerning the warning signs in recent years understands that white Christian fundamentalism is odiously responsible for enabling and even championing the shredding of the fabric of American democracy.

If you are in the process of healing the evangelical wound within yourself or if you still identify as evangelical, compassionately and kindly understand that healing the wound is not strictly a personal matter. Millions of other individuals carry the same wound, as well as a host of cultures around the world that have been irreparably damaged by fundamentalist missionary efforts. Dominionism exacts a terrible price, but it is possible to attend to your own healing and also actively oppose authoritarianism in its many forms whenever and wherever you observe it. You need not do this alone, nor should you. A host of supportive resources exist that did not when I was exiting Christian fundamentalism fifty years ago.

The philosopher Blaise Pascal wrote that "men never do evil so completely and cheerfully as when they do it from religious conviction."[37] Thousands of years before Pascal, Hippocrates admonished his students to "do no harm." Christian fundamentalism is not the only enabler of democracy's demise. As a host of factors are playing out simultaneously to shred the last remaining fibers of democracy from Mar a Lago to Myanmar—as we all recover from religious trauma and the impacts of authoritarian influences in our lives, we have a moral obligation to discern fact from fiction, accuracy from conspiracy theory, and to disentangle our devotion from dogma.

ACKNOWLEDGMENTS

In publishing a book outside the genre in which I usually write, I have been vigorously supported by so many associates. I want to express my heartfelt appreciation to my Apocryphile publisher, John Mabry and his staff for taking the risk and being willing to experiment. I am humbled and honored by a stunning foreword from Frank Schaeffer whom I have considered a spiritual sibling for years. We have survived and are thriving! Thank you Andrew Harvey for your love and support in our past writing partnership and beyond. Gratitude to you Terry Chapman for your support and your incessant willingness to conspire with me in making radical mischief. I extend my deepest gratitude to Richard Rohr, Matthew Fox, Jim Finley, Mirabai Starr, and Pema Chodron whose teachings have been invaluable disinfectants in eradicating the subtle influences of toxic fundamentalism decades after "leaving the fold." Thank you Dr. Marlene Winell for your uncanny mirroring of my story as you shamelessly tell yours and dedicate your career to assisting religious trauma survivors in their healing. Thank you Deborah for your love and longsuffering in living with a survivor of fundamentalist abuse. Thank you Shana, Janis, and the two Kathleen's in my life. Thank you Daphne for your spiritual guidance and undying faith in me and all that makes me alive. Gratitude to all living beings on this planet and beyond who have guided and protected me all these decades. You are the reason for my being. I owe you my life and my work.

NOTES

INTRODUCTION

1. Sarah Posner, *Unholy: Why White Evangelicals Worship At The Altar of Donald Trump*, Random House, 2020, Introduction, p.10.
2. "New Survey Shows 3 In 5 White Evangelicals Say Joe Biden Wasn't Legitimately Elected," NPR, February, 2021, https://www.npr.org/2021/02/19/969351648/new-survey-shows-3-in-5-white-evangelicals-say-joe-biden-wasnt-legitimately-elec
3. "QAnon Now as Popular in U.S. as Some Major Religions, Poll Suggests," *New York Times*, May 27, 2021.
4. *UK Independent*, "QAnon has merged with white Christian evangelicals, experts say—and the results could be lethal," Andrew Feinberg, March, 2021, https://www.independent.co.uk/voices/qanon-march-4-white-christian-evangelicals-b1812490.html
5. Steven Levitsky, Daniel Ziblatt, *How Democracies Die*, Crown Publishing, 2018, p.5.
6. "Historian wonders: Is Joe Biden 'a speed bump on the fascists' march to power'?" Alternet, Chauncey DeVega, May 26, 2021, https://www.alternet.org/2021/05/historian-wonders-is-joe-biden-a-speed-bump-on-the-fascists-march-to-power/

1. UNDERSTANDING CRISTOFASCISM

1. "Trump And The Christian Fascists," Chris Hedges, Truthdig, July 24, 2017, https://www.truthdig.com/articles/trump-and-the-christian-fascists/
2. "The Debate over the word 'fascism' takes a new turn," Jennifer Szalai, *New York Times*, June 10, 2020.
3. "Yale Professor Jason Stanley Identifies 3 Essential Features of Fascism: Invoking a Mythic Past, Sowing Division & Attacking Truth," Open Culture, October 25, 2018, https://www.openculture.com/2018/10/yale-professor-jason-stanley-identifies-three-essential-features-of-fascism.html
4. "Footage Recalls the Night Madison Square Garden Filled With Nazis," *Smithsonian Magazine*, October 13, 2017, https://www.smithsonianmag.com/smart-news/documentary-shows-1939-nazi-rally-madison-square-garden-180965248/
5. *Ibid.*
6. Kali Holloway, "Trump Is an Eerily Perfect Match With a Famous 14-Point Guide to Identify Fascist Leaders," Alternet, December 6, 2016) http://

171

www.alternet.org/election-2016/trump-eerily-perfect-match-famous-14-point-guide-identify-fascist-leaders

7. "Fascism is Not an Idea to Be Debated, It's a Set of Actions to Fight," Aleksandar Hemon, Literary Hub, November 1, 2018, https://lithub.com/fascism-is-not-an-idea-to-be-debated-its-a-set-of-actions-to-fight/?fbclid=IwAR3mZRhlJRcFl8D4iqyLW8ioBzH-l0fjiIwP7d0KTitht3QlVxVevYx9Pc4

8. "America is at a fascist turning point—and only totally disempowering and humiliating Trump will stop it," Thom Hartmann, Medium, January 17, 2021, https://thomhartmann.medium.com/america-is-at-a-fascist-turning-point-and-only-totally-disempowering-and-humiliating-trump-will-9106154de199

9. "Republicans' efforts to end the American republic makes them Republicans in name only," Robert McElvaine, NBC News, January 6, 2021, https://www.nbcnews.com/think/opinion/republicans-efforts-end-american-republic-makes-them-republicans-name-only-ncna1252872

10. Bill Moyers on Democracy, https://billmoyers.com/story/coronavirus-voting-rights-election-gerrymandering/

11. Christofascism, Paul Tillich, https://en.google-info.org/index.php/27020111/1/christofascism.html

12. Frances Fitzgerald, *The Evangelicals*, Simon & Schuster, 2017, Glossary

13. Wikipedia, "Biblical Literalism," https://en.wikipedia.org/wiki/Biblical_literalism

14. *Ibid.*

15. Bart Ehrman: *Misquoting Jesus: The Story Behind Who Changed The Bible And Why*, Harper Collins, 2005, p. 202-207.

16. View from an Open Rectory Window, Reverend Roger quoting Marcus Borg, https://viewfromanopenrectorywindow.wordpress.com/2015/01/29/marcus-borg-r-i-p/

17. "The Day Christian Fundamentalism Was Born," Matthew Avery Sutton, *New York Times*, May 25, 2019, https://www.nytimes.com/2019/05/25/opinion/the-day-christian-fundamentalism-was-born.html

18. *Ibid.*

19. Carl Jung, *Aion* (1951). Collected Works 9, Part II: P.14

2. RACE, GENDER, AND THE PROSPERITY GOSPEL

1. *The Life of Frederick Douglass*, p. 119.

2. "Creflo Dollar's ministry says he will get his $65 million jet," *Atlanta Journal Constitution*, September 23, 2016, https://www.ajc.com/news/local/creflo-dollar-ministry-says-will-get-his-million-jet/Z1Oa81oGK9BYz1LO4KswAK/

3. Frances Fitzgerald, *The Evangelicals*, p.76.

4. *White Evangelical Racism*, Anthea Butler, University of North Carolina Press, https://uncpress.org/book/9781469661179/white-evangelical-racism/
5. Robert Jones, *White Too Long: The Legacy of White Supremacy in American Christianity*, Simon & Schuster, 2020, p.5.
6. *Ibid*, p. 70.
7. *Ibid.*, p. 94.
8. "The Real Origins of the Religious Right," Randall Balmer, *Politico*, May 27, 2014, https://www.politico.com/magazine/story/2014/05/religious-right-real-origins-107133/
9. "White Evangelical Racism Has Always Been a Political Power Grab," Sarah Stankorb, Medium, April 7, 2021, https://gen.medium.com/white-evangelical-racism-has-always-been-a-political-power-grab-7390c8f0d4ee
10. Robert Jones, *White Too Long*, p. 96.
11. *Ibid.*, p. 100.
12. "Feminists and their perspectives on the church fathers' beliefs regarding women: An inquiry," Hannelie Wood, http://www.scielo.org.za/scielo.php?script=sci_arttext&pid=S2074-77052017000100005
13. "Beth Moore, A Prominent Evangelical, Splits With Southern Baptists, https://www.nytimes.com/2021/03/10/us/beth-moore-southern-baptists.html?smid=em-share
14. *Ibid.*
15. "Pro-Trump prophet goes on wild rant, says the modern church is 'almost homosexual,'" *Business Insider*, April 12, 2021, https://www.insider.com/pro-trump-prophet-says-the-modern-church-is-almost-homosexual-2021-4
16. "The Shocking Net Worth of These 10 Richest U.S. Pastors Will Blow Your Mind," https://www.cheatsheet.com/entertainment/net-worth-richest-pastors-will-blow-your-mind.html/
17. *Ibid.*
18. Frances Fitzgerald, *The Evangelicals*, p. 106.
19. Mary Hammond, "God's Business Men: Entrepreneurial Evangelicals in Depression and War," A Dissertation Presented to the Faculty of the Graduate School of Yale University, 2010.
20. *Ibid.*

3. THE PSYCHOLOGY OF CONTEMPORARY CHRISTIAN FUNDAMENTALISM

1. Marlene Winell, *Leaving the Fold: A Guide for Former Fundamentalists and Others Leaving Their Religion* Apocryphile Press, p. 17, Kindle Edition.
2. "The Fundamentalist Moment," *Commonweal Magazine* Peter Schwendener, February 18, 2011, https://www.commonwealmagazine.org/fundamentalist-moment
3. Original Sin, Wikipedia, https://en.wikipedia.org/wiki/Original_sin

4. Tertullian, *De Cultu Feminarium* (*On the Apparel of Women*), Chapter 1, https://margmowczko.com/misogynist-quotes-from-church-fathers/
5. Augustine, Letter to Laetus, 243.10, https://margmowczko.com/misogynist-quotes-from-church-fathers/
6. Martin Luther, *Commentary on Genesis*, Chapter 2, Part V, 27b., https://margmowczko.com/misogynist-quotes-from-church-fathers/
7.
8. "The Church Needs Shame to Function, Dan Foster, Medium, December, 23, 2020, https://medium.com/backyard-theology/the-church-needs-shame-to-function-21b72bb88358
9.
10. Good Faith Media, John Pierce, May 25, 2018, https://goodfaithmedia.org/certainty-is-root-of-all-fundamentalist-problems/
11. Helen Elerbee, *The Dark Side of Christian History*, Morningstar and Lark Publications, 1995, p.139.
12. Frivolities of Courtiers and Footprints of Philosophers, Sir John of Salisbury, https://constitution.org/2-Authors/salisbury/policrat123.htm
13. "The evangelical presidency: Reagan's dangerous love affair with the Christian right," Steven Miller, *Salon*, May 18, 2014, https://www.salon.com/2014/05/18/the_evangelical_presidency_reagans_dangerous_love_affair_with_the_christian_right/
14. "Pentecostalism," Wikipedia, https://en.wikipedia.org/wiki/Pentecostalism
15. "Why Do These Pentecostals Keep Growing?" *Christianity Today*, November 11, 2014, https://www.christianitytoday.com/edstetzer/2014/november/why-are-pentecostals-growing.html
16. "Religious Trauma Syndrome," Marlene Winell, https://journeyfree.org/rts/
17. Broadview, "Former fundamentalists describe the trauma of leaving their faith," https://broadview.org/former-fundamentalists-describe-the-trauma-of-leaving-their-faith/
18. Trump-loving MyPillow CEO looking for evidence of Satanism in Trump's election loss," Brad Reed, Raw Story, March, 2021, https://www.rawstory.com/mike-lindell-2651168602/
19. Kristin Kobes Du Mez, *Jesus and John Wayne: How White Evangelicals Corrupted a Faith and Fractured a Nation*, Liveright, 2020, p. 19.

4. BRING THEM IN FROM THE FIELDS OF SIN

1. "What is the Difference Between Fundamentalists and Evangelicals?" What Christians Want To Know, https://www.whatchristianswanttoknow.com/what-is-the-difference-between-fundamentalists-and-evangelicals/
2. "Christian Missions," Wikipedia, https://en.wikipedia.org/wiki/Christian_mission

3. "Thy Will Be Done," *Kirkus Review of Books*, https://www.kirkusreviews. com/book-reviews/gerard-colby/thy-will-be-done/
4. *Los Angeles Times Review of Books*, 1995, https://www.latimes.com/archives/ la-xpm-1995-05-14-bk-273-story.html
5. *Ibid.*
6. "A Political Warning Shot: 'American Theocracy'," NPR, March, 2006, https://www.npr.org/2006/03/21/5290373/a-political-warning-shot-american-theocracy
7. "Chris Hedges on "American Fascists: The Christian Right and the War on America," *Democracy Now*, February 19, 2007, https://www.democracynow. org/2007/2/19/chris_hedges_on_american_fascists_the

5. EVANGELICAL POLITICS

1. "The Evil Within Us," Chris Hedges, *Scheer Post*, March 22, 2021, https:// scheerpost.com/2021/03/22/hedges-the-evil-within-us/
2. David Trowbridge, *United States History, Vol 2*, Flatworld, 2021
3. "How George H.W. Bush enabled the rise of the religious right," Neil Young, *Washington Post*, December 5, 2018, https://www.washingtonpost.com/ outlook/2018/12/05/how-george-hw-bush-enabled-rise-religious-right/
4. "The Family: The Secret Fundamentalism At The Heart of American Power," Jeff Sharlet, Kirkus Review, June 1, 2008, https://www. kirkusreviews.com/book-reviews/jeff-sharlet/the-family-2/
5. *Google Books Review*, "The Family: Power, Politics and Fundamentalism's Shadow Elite," My Book
6. Mitchell, Andrea; Popkin, James 'Jim' (April 3, 2008). "Political ties to a secretive religious group". NBC News. Retrieved January 28, 2010.
7. "The Family: inside the sinister sect that has infected western democracy," *The Guardian*, Jack Seale, August 15, 2019, https://www.theguardian.com/ tv-and-radio/2019/aug/15/the-family-netflix-powerful-sinister-christian-sect-trump
8. "What *The Family* Reveals About White Evangelicals, Donald Trump, and the 'Wolf King,'" *Vulture*, Sarah Jones, August 29, 2019, https://www. vulture.com/2019/08/the-family-netflix-trump-white-evangelicals.html
9. "The biblical story the Christian right uses to defend Trump," Tara Isabella Burton, *Vox*, March 5, 2018, https://www.vox.com/identities/2018/3/5/ 16796892/trump-cyrus-christian-right-bible-cbn-evangelical-propaganda
10. "'Allergic reaction to US religious right' fueling decline of religion, experts say," *The Guardian*, April 5, 2021, https://www.theguardian.com/world/ 2021/apr/05/americans-religion-rightwing-politics-decline
11. "How the decline of religion is radicalizing the evangelical right," Alex Henderson, Alternet, April 1, 2021, https://www.alternet.org/2021/04/ religion-in-us-politics/?utm_source=&utm_medium=email& utm_campaign=6888

12. "It Is Time To Talk About Violent Christian Extremism," Elizabeth Neumann, *Politico*, February 4, 2021, https://www.politico.com/news/magazine/2021/02/04/qanon-christian-extremism-nationalism-violence-466034
13. *Ibid.*
14. *Democracy Now*, Chris Hedges & Amy Goodman, February 19, 2007, https://www.democracynow.org/2007/2/19/chris_hedges_on_american_fascists_the
15. *Ibid.*
16. "The Nine Mysteries of The Prayer Shawl," John Hagee, https://www.youtube.com/watch?v=bwFCbKosZ4g

6. A LITTLE KNOWLEDGE IS A DANGEROUS THING

1. *The Jung-White Letters*, p.285.
2. Anne Frank, *The Diary of A Young Girl*, 1947, p. 11.
3. Edward L. Jackson, Wikipedia, https://en.wikipedia.org/wiki/Edward_L._Jackson
4. "A Deep Dive Into Religious Trauma Syndrome," Dr. Marlene Winell, YouTube, March 27, 2020, https://www.youtube.com/watch?v=G96qz_TUzBc
5. "A Pastor's Son Becomes a Critic of Religion on TikTok," *New York Times*, Ruth Graham, April 12, 2021, https://www.nytimes.com/2021/04/12/us/abraham-piper-tiktok-exvangelical.html?action=click&module=In%20Other%20News&pgtype=Homepage
6. Frank Schaeffer, *Why I Am An Atheist Who Believes In God,"* My Book
7. "The Perennial Tradition," Richard Rohr, December 20, 2015, *The Center for Action and Contemplation*, https://cac.org/the-perennial-tradition-2015-12-20/
8. *The World Wisdom Bible: A New Testament For A Global Spirituality*, Edited by Rami Shapiro, Perennial Wisdom for The Spiritually Independent, Sky Light Paths, 2017, Introduction.
9. *Ibid.*, Introduction.
10. *Ibid.*, Introduction.
11. Matthew Fox, *Original Blessing*, Bear Publishing, Santa Fe, 1983, p.49.
12. Paul Maxwell, *The Trauma of Doctrine: New Calvinism, Religious Abuse, and the Experience of God*, Fortress Academic Press, 2021, Preface.

7. HEALING THE EVANGELICAL WOUND: RESTORING THE SOUL

1. Michael Meade, *Awakening The Soul*, Greenfire Press, 2018, p. 21.
2. "Recovery From Harmful Religion," Dr. Marlene Winell website, http://marlenewinell.net/recovery-
3. "Vanished From the Earth," Joshua Rivera, *Slate Magazine*, May 2, 2021, https://slate.com/human-interest/2021/05/rapture-fear-evangelical-americans-church-miller.html
4. "Recovery From Harmful Religion, Marlene Winell".
5. Journey Free Support Group, Dr. Marlene Winell, https://journeyfree.org/group-forum/
6. Recovering From Religion, "Healing From Religious Harm," https://www.recoveringfromreligion.org/religious-resources
7. "One of America's top climate scientists is an evangelical Christian. She's on a mission to persuade skeptics," Dan Zak, *Washington Post*, July 15, 2019, https://www.washingtonpost.com/lifestyle/style/one-of-americas-top-climate-scientists-is-an-evangelical-christian-shes-on-a-mission-to-convert-skeptics/2019/07/12/9018094c-8d2a-11e9-adf3-f70f78c156e8_story.html
8. Marlene Winell, *Leaving the Fold: A Guide for Former Fundamentalists and Others Leaving Their Religion*, Apocryphile Press, January, 2006, Preface.
9. Mark Nepo, *The Book of Awakening: Having the Life You Want by Being Present to the Life You Have*, Red Wheel, 2020, p.94.

8. CONFRONTING KU KLUX CHRISTIANITY

1. "The Feynman Series," You Tube, October 2, 2011, https://www.youtube.com/watch?v=cRmbwczTC6E
2. "The good White Christian women of Nazi Germany," D.L. Mayfield, *Christian Century*, March 25, 2021, https://www.christiancentury.org/article/critical-essay/good-white-christian-women-nazi-germany?fbclid=IwAR3D4Xc-DFdPop22lkKaVIBm-L-7P1gtPPdmEad5M-TkY3kbG9wT0_pEXJ8
3. Richard Rohr, *The Universal Christ: How a Forgotten Reality Can Change Everything We See, Hope For, and Believe*, Convergent Books, 2021, p. 127.
4. "Author Traces Christianity's Path From 'Forbidden Religion' To A 'Triumph,'" NPR, Terry Gross interviews Bart Ehrman, March 20, 2018, https://www.npr.org/transcripts/595161200
5. "What Is Critical Thinking?" University of Hong Kong, https://philosophy.hku.hk/think/critical/ct.php
6. Wikipedia, "White Privilege," https://en.wikipedia.org/wiki/White_privilege

7. "White Evangelical Racism Has Always Been a Political Power Grab," Sarah Stankorb, *The Conversation*, April, 2021, https://gen.medium.com/white-evangelical-racism-has-always-been-a-political-power-grab-7390c8f0d4ee

8. "Evangelical pundit started "White History Month" to replace Pride Month for Christians," *LGBTQ Nation*, June 4, 2021, https://www.lgbtqnation.com/2021/06/evangelical-pundit-started-white-history-month-replace-pride-month-christians/

9. "WHO ARE THE LATINO EVANGELICALS THAT SUPPORT TRUMP?" Aaron Sanchez, *Sojourners*, November 26, 2019, https://sojo.net/articles/who-are-latino-evangelicals-support-trump

10. "Christians Should Rule This Country And Take It By Force," *Friendly Atheist Website*, April, 2021, https://friendlyatheist.patheos.com/2021/04/21/hate-preacher-christians-should-rule-this-country-and-take-it-by-force/?utm_medium=email&utm_source=BRSS&utm_campaign=Nonreligious&utm_content=361&fbclid=IwAR0JAwG7PJtOuYwAeA29-Z6G2C1Y1Tdcyuhjlji8JabLu1xBC6Bwuwu9Rwg

11. "Handmaid's Tale," https://en.wikipedia.org/wiki/The_Handmaid%27s_Tale_(TV_series)

12. New Apostolic Reformation, Wikipedia, https://en.wikipedia.org/wiki/New_Apostolic_Reformation

13. "The New Apostolic Reformation and the Theology of Prosperity: The 'Kingdom of God' as a Hermeneutical Key," Laussane Movement, https://lausanne.org/content/88558

14. *Ibid.*

15. "How the Christian Right Helped Foment Insurrection," Sarah Posner, *Rolling Stone*, January 31, 2021, https://www.rollingstone.com/culture/culture-features/capitol-christian-right-trump-1121236/

16. *Ibid.*

17. "I'm a Climate Scientist Who Believes in God. Hear Me Out," *New York Times*, Katherine Hayhoe, October 31, 2019, https://www.nytimes.com/2019/10/31/opinion/sunday/climate-change-evangelical-christian.html

18. "Exploring anti-science attitudes among political and Christian conservatives through an examination of American universities on Twitter," https://www.tandfonline.com/doi/full/10.1080/23311886.2018.1462134

19. *New York Times*, April 5, 2021, https://www.nytimes.com/2021/04/05/world/millions-of-white-evangelicals-do-not-intend-to-get-vaccinated.html

20. "What a Real President Was Like," Bill Moyers, *Washington Post*, Nov 13, 1988, https://www.washingtonpost.com/archive/opinions/1988/11/13/what-a-real-president-was-like/d483c1be-d0da-43b7-bde6-04e10106ff6c/

21. "Why QAnon Has Attracted So Many White Evangelicals," Kaleigh Rogers, *Five-Thirty-Eight*, March 4, 2021, https://fivethirtyeight.com/features/why-qanon-has-attracted-so-many-white-evangelicals/

22. *Ibid.*

23. "Acclaimed Journalist and Alumnus Speaks on Trump and Christian Fascism," *Colgate Maroon News*, February 27, 2020, https://thecolgatemaroonnews.com/704/news/acclaimed-journalist-and-alumnus-speaks-on-trump-and-christian-fascism/

24. Gordon Thomas, Greg Lewis, *Defying Hitler: The Germans Who Resisted Nazi Rule*, Random House, 2019, p.7.

25. German Evangelical Church (Reich Church) Wikipedia, https://en.wikipedia.org/wiki/German_Evangelical_Church

26. *Ibid*, https://en.wikipedia.org/wiki/Dietrich_Bonhoeffer

27. "The Scandal Rocking The Evangelical World, *Atlantic Magazine*, Peter Wehner, June 7, 2021, https://www.theatlantic.com/ideas/archive/2021/06/russell-moore-sbc/619122/

28. *Ibid*.

29. Every Day in America, Dick Gregory, https://everydayinamerica.blog/tag/dick-gregory/

30. Benjamin Corey website, https://www.benjaminlcorey.com/how-to-completely-misuse-the-bible-in-5-easy-steps/

31. "'Evangelical' Is Not a Religious Identity. It's a Political One," *Atlantic Magazine Podcast*, May 13, 2021, https://www.theatlantic.com/podcasts/archive/2021/05/evangelicals-republican-voters/618845/?utm_source=newsletter&utm_medium=email&utm_campaign=atlantic-daily-newsletter&utm_content=20210514&silverid=%%RECIPIENT_ID%%&utm_term=The%20Atlantic%20Daily

32. "Revealed: $280m 'dark money' spent by US Christian right groups globally," *Open Democracy Website*, October 27, 2020, https://www.opendemocracy.net/en/5050/trump-us-christian-spending-global-revealed/

33. "White Supremacist Christianity Drives Trump's Loyal Mob. We Must Scream It Down," George Yancy, *Truthout*, https://truthout.org/articles/white-supremacist-christianity-drives-trumps-loyal-mob-we-must-scream-it-down/

34. "More than a quarter of white evangelicals believe core QAnon conspiracy theory," Religious News Service, February 11, 2021, https://religionnews.com/2021/02/11/survey-more-than-a-quarter-of-white-evangelicals-believe-core-qanon-conspiracy-theory/

35. "Billy Graham's granddaughter: Evangelical leaders are failing us by supporting Trump," *The Hill*, August 25, 2020, https://thehill.com/homenews/administration/513577-billy-grahams-granddaughter-evangelical-leaders-are-failing-us-by

36. "QAnon has merged with white Christian evangelicals, experts say—and the results could be lethal," *UK Independent*, March 4, 2021, https://www.independent.co.uk/voices/qanon-march-4-white-christian-evangelicals-b1812490.html

37. Blaise Pascal, *Pensees*, 1670.

ABOUT THE AUTHOR

Carolyn Baker, Ph.D., was a psychotherapist in private practice for 17 years and a professor of psychology and history for 10. She is the author of 13 books including *Navigating The Coming Chaos: A Handbook For Inner Transition; Sacred Demise: Walking The Spiritual Path of Industrial Civilization's Collapse*; and *Love In The Age of Ecological Apocalypse*. She has also co-authored 4 books with Andrew Harvey. She manages her website at www. carolynbaker.net and publishes a subscription-based Daily News Digest which is a collection of news stories and inspiration focusing on the global crisis and options for navigating disruptive times. Carolyn offers life coaching and spiritual counseling in Boulder, Colorado and worldwide for people who want help with dealing with the unprecedented challenges of our time.

Leaving the Fold
A Guide for Former Fundamentalists
and Others Leaving Their Religion

This book by psychologist Marlene Winell provides valuable insights into the dangers of religious indoctrination and outlines what therapists and victims can do to reclaim a healthier human spirit.... Both former believers searching for a new beginning and those just starting to subject their faith to the requirements of simple common sense, if not analytical reason, may find valuable assistance in these pages.

—Steve Allen, author and entertainer

Leaving the Fold is a unique and invaluable guide to the psychological harm done by Christian fundamentalism. Dr. Winell's book is practical, relevant, and altogether real.

—Dr. Edmund Cohen, author of *The Mind of the Bible Believer*

Leaving the Fold is invaluable to those who have gone through the ordeal of religious addiction, abuse, and disillusionment, and who need a recovery plan. I highly recommend this book not only to the wounded, but also urge all pastors to study it carefully and then re-assess their own ministries. Dr. Marlene Winell has made a most important contribution to deal with the most heart-wrenching of experiences.

—Rev. Austin Miles, author of *Don't Call Me Brother* and *Setting the Captives Free*

Read *Leaving the Fold* today!
https://books2read.com/leavingthefold

Toxic Jesus
A Journey from Holy Shit to Spiritual Healing

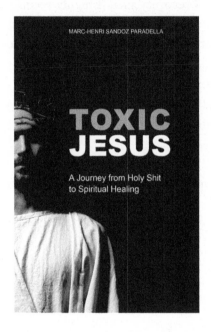

Do religion and spirituality bring up feelings of guilt, shame, and abuse?

Uncover the dark power of toxic spirituality and its lingering influence on your life... and learn how to heal from it and access a new intimacy with yourself and a renewed, free and life-sustaining spirituality.

Toxic Jesus is a thought-provoking book rooted in the author's deep personal experience. It shows how every religion can become toxic and promote shame, guilt and repression. It exposes how the poison of toxic spirituality hides behind religious façades and affects every person exposed to it.

Finally, it guides you through the path of recovering from the damages caused by toxic spirituality.

Toxic Jesus is the eye-opener you need to reconsider your spiritual history. It will help you to transmute the poison of toxic spirituality into healing and growth.

Buy *Toxic Jesus* today!
https://books2read.com/toxicjesus

Made in the USA
Monee, IL
10 August 2022